A HANDBOOK OF
CREATIVE
CHORAL
SPEAKING

by

Marjory Frances Brown-Azarowicz

Associate Professor
George Mason College of
the University of Virginia

Burgess Publishing Company

426 South Sixth Street • Minneapolis, Minn. 55415

Educational Consultant to Publisher:
Leo E. Eastman
Head, Department of Education and Psychology,
Illinois State University,
Normal, Illinois

808.55
B881h

Copyright © 1970 by Burgess Publishing Company
All rights reserved
Printed in the United States of America
Library of Congress Catalog Card Number 73-102135
Standard Book Number 8087-0259-9

DEDICATED

to my parents

Charles and Isobella Brown

PREFACE

A Handbook of Creative Choral Speaking was planned as a book of methodology for teachers and includes ways in which choral speaking has been taught since its inception into the language arts program in the 1920's.

Here is a variety of methods, some old, some new, some used in American schools, and some used in English schools, balanced by the writer's personal views of how a teacher may adapt the varying and sometimes conflicting methods of choral speaking to individual classes and individual teacher needs.

Stress has been placed upon teacher and student creativity within the framework of the mechanical techniques of traditional choral speaking. The text does not suggest that technique be discarded. The techniques of choral speaking are the framework upon which creativity in choral speaking develops. This framework must be overlaid with a well-developed language arts program in which children's poetic and speaking abilities grow and flourish.

This is the first compilation of the methodology of the major writers from the 1920's onward. Much of the research is gathered in Chapter IV, "Metrical Emphasis in Choral Speaking," Chapter VII, "Your Orchestral Score," and Chapter VIII, "Your Magic Wand."

It is hoped that the experienced teacher will gain new ideas from Chapter XII and that the beginning teacher will be inspired by Chapters V and III, and that all teachers will try in some measure to lead their students to the land of the Pied Piper.

The writer wishes to express her thanks to the graduate students at the State University of New York, College at Buffalo, who suggested the text, and to the hundreds of children in the public schools of Calgary, Alberta, Canada, who helped her through the years to synthesize a method in choral speaking which has proved sound and practical in classroom situations.

Marjory F. Brown-Azarowicz

TABLE OF CONTENTS

		Page
Preface		v
Acknowledgments		ix

Chapter
I.	Introduction	1
II.	Backgrounds of Choral Speaking	5
III.	The Pied Piper	11
IV.	Metrical Emphasis in Choral Speaking	21
V.	The Beginning Teacher	29
VI.	Choice of Choral Speaking Selections	53
VII.	Your Orchestral Score	65
	Differing Notational Formats	65
	Simple Notations	66
	Detailed Notations	70
	Prose Notations	71
VIII.	Your Magic Wand	81
	The Attack and Release	94
IX.	Talking Together in the Classroom	101
	Class Organization	101
	Memorization	106

	Oral Reading Skills 108
	Creativity in Choral Speaking 110
X.	Voice Production 115
	Breathing Techniques 116
	Speech Difficulties 117
XI.	The Curtain Rises 127
XII.	Techniques for the Advanced Choir 133
	The Choir 134
	The Mechanics of Interpretation................135
	Tonal Qualities 140

Bibliography 145

ACKNOWLEDGMENTS

"Aeroplane," Chapter V, by Mary McB. Green, from *ANOTHER HERE AND NOW STORY BOOK* by Lucy Sprague Mitchell. Copyright 1937 by E.P. Dutton and Co., Inc., renewed 1965 by Lucy Sprague Mitchell. Reprinted by permission of E.P. Dutton & Co., Inc.

"The Day Will Bring Some Lovely Thing," Chapter IX, by Grace Noll Crowell, from *POEMS OF INSPIRATION AND COURAGE* by Grace Noll Crowell. Copyright 1928, 1934 by Harper & Brothers, renewed 1956, 1962 by Grace Noll Crowell. Reprinted by permission of Harper and Row, Publishers.

"Evening Hymn," Chapter VIII, by Elizabeth Madox Roberts, from *SONG IN THE MEADOW* by Elizabeth Madox Roberts. Copyright 1940 by Elizabeth Madox Roberts, renewed 1968 by Ivor S. Roberts. Reprinted by permission of The Viking Press.

"Ferry Boats," Chapter IX, by James S. Tippett, from *I GO A-TRAVELLING* by James S. Tippett. Copyright 1929 by Harper & Brothers, renewed 1957 by James S. Tippett. Reprinted by permission of Harper & Row, Publishers.

"Higgledy-Piggledy," Chapter VIII, by Kate Greenaway, from *UNDER THE WINDOW* by Kate Greenaway. Copyright 1879 by Frederick Warne & Co., Limited. Reprinted by permission of F. Warne & Co., Inc.

"I'm Hiding," Chapter VIII, by Dorothy Aldis, from *EVERYTHING AND ANYTHING* by Dorothy Aldis. Copyright 1925, 1926, 1927 by Dorothy Aldis. Reprinted by permission of G. P. Putnam's Sons.

"Indian Children," Chapter IX, by Annette Wynne, from *FOR DAYS AND DAYS* by Annette Wynne. Copyright 1919, 1947 by Annette Wynne. Reprinted by permission of J.B.Lippincott Co.

"I Never Saw a Moor," Chapter VIII, by Emily Dickinson, from *THE POEMS OF EMILY DICKINSON* edited by Thomas H. Johnson. Copyright 1951, 1955 by the President and Fellows of Harvard College. Reprinted by permission of The Belknap Press of Harvard University Press and the Trustees of Amherst College.

"Jonathan Bing Visits the King," Chapter V, by Beatrice Curtis Brown, from *JONATHAN BING* by Beatrice Curtis Brown. Copyright 1936 by Oxford University Press, renewed 1964 by Beatrice Curtis Brown. Reprinted by permission of Lothrop, Lee & Shepard Co., Inc.

"Lincoln," Chapter III, by Nancy Byrd Turner, from *CHILD LIFE*. Copyright by Nancy Byrd Turner. Reprinted by permission of Nancy Byrd Turner.

"The Lullaby of the Iroquois," Chapter V, by E. Pauline Johnson, from *FLINT AND FEATHER* by E. Pauline Johnson. Copyright 1931 by Hodder & Stoughton, Ltd., Toronto, Canada. Reprinted by permission of Hodder and Stoughton, Ltd., Toronto, Canada.

"Mary Middling," Chapter III, by Rose Fyleman, from *NEW NURSERY RHYMES* by Rose Fyleman. Copyright 1932 by Doubleday & Company, Inc. Reprinted by permission of Doubleday & Company, Inc.

"Mrs. Peck-Pigeon," Chapter IV, by Eleanor Farjeon, from *POEMS FOR CHILDREN* by Eleanor Farjeon. Copyright 1933 and 1961 by Eleanor Farjeon. Reprinted by permission of J.B. Lippincott Co.

"Night Plane," Chapter V, by Frances Frost, from *NEW YORK HERALD TRIBUNE,* May 1956. Copyright by Frances Frost. Reprinted by permission of N. Carr Grace.

"The Old Log House," Chapter IV, by James S. Tippett, from *A WORLD TO KNOW* by James S. Tippett. Copyright 1933 by Harper & Brothers, renewed 1961 by Martha K. Tippett. Reprinted by permission of Harper & Row, Publishers.

"School Is Over," Chapter IX, by Kate Greenaway, from *UNDER THE WINDOW* by Kate Greenaway. Copyright 1879 by Frederick Warne & Co., Limited. Reprinted by permission of F. Warne & Co., Inc.

"The Scissor-Man," Chapter XII, by Madeline Nightingale, from *NURSERY LAYS FOR NURSERY DAYS* by Madeline Nightingale. Copyright by Basil Blackwell & Mott Ltd. Reprinted by permission of Basil Blackwell & Mott Ltd.

"Silver," Chapter VII, by Walter de la Mare. Reprinted by permission of The Literary Trustees of Walter de la Mare and The Society of Authors as their representative.

"Silver Ships," Chapter V, by Mildred Plew Meigs, from *CHILD LIFE.* Reprinted by permission of Marion Ruckel.

"The Song My Paddle Sings," Chapter IX, by E. Pauline Johnson, from *FLINT AND FEATHER* by E. Pauline Johnson. Copyright 1931 by Hodder & Stoughton, Ltd., Toronto, Canada. Reprinted by permission of Hodder & Stoughton, Ltd., Toronto, Canada.

"Up in the Air," Chapter V, by James S. Tippett, from *I GO A-TRAVELLING* by James S. Tippett. Copyright 1929 by Harper & Brothers, renewed 1957 by James S. Tippett. Reprinted by permission of Harper & Row, Publishers.

In some cases where poems have not been acknowledged, I have searched diligently to find the sources and to obtain permission to use the poems, but without success. M.B-A.

"He who reads a poem well

is also a poet"

Ralph Waldo Emerson

Chapter I
INTRODUCTION

To the human ear nothing is more soul-stirring than the tones of a resonant voice speaking or singing messages of deep human emotion. An infant is first stirred to utilize his own speech organs by all the sounds of the human voices he hears about him — the comforting lullabies — the tones of endearment. The child is aroused by the jingle of nursery rhymes and the wonders of story time; youth by great ideas in spoken as well as written literature; the loved-one by simple endearments; the mob by cries of the rabble rousers; the political rally by the voice of the politician; and parents by a telephone call across a continent.

Some voices are beautiful, some raucous, some soft, some beguiling, but all arouse in the listener's mind man's great urge to communicate, to express ideas "trippingly on the tongue."[1] Each individual desires freedom to express himself to others. Babies express this desire by imitation. They copy patterns of language. They listen carefully and gradually develop individual patterns of language. The individual needs freedom to express himself. He needs freedom to grow and develop discrimination and taste in oral and written language. He needs to grow in his knowledge and desire to speak and write and read, to explore the patterns of language, and to develop fluency and ease in oral and written communication skills.

The urge to communicate is one of man's strongest urges. There is power in this urge. Power to change lives and ideas. Upon this urge and power we may capitalize.

This book deals with one phase of man's oral communication, choral speaking. Through choral speaking individuals and groups can come to learn and understand the power and beauty of the human voice and written literature and gain the freedom necessary to grow in personal language skills.

Choral speaking is group oral interpretation of literature. It is a social activity and needs listeners as well as speakers. In choral speaking "many minds understand and many voices express the same idea and shade of emotion at the same instant."[2]

This book is written for both novice and accomplished choral speaking leaders and endeavors to present basic ideas from the literature of choral speaking and to show the reader how to pick and choose from these many ideas in order to meet the needs of particular situations. It is based upon the premise that the ultimate in true choral speaking techniques is the ability of groups of students to develop creative interpretations of the selections studied.

For many years the methods of formal elocution were used in oral reading, public speaking, and choral speaking. This is no longer true. Today oral communication stresses meaning. Oral communication is person-to-person expressions of understandings and meaning. It is truth-seeking realized through non-rigid approaches. Each individual or group of individuals is free to interpret the writings of others according to individual feelings, moods, and understandings. Choral speaking has developed into personal and group interpretations of thoughts and ideas. Each member of the choral speaking choir becomes not only creator, but poet as well.

The purposes of the book may be stated as follows:

1. To encourage wider use of choral speaking in schools and with youth groups.
2. To present basic steps in choral speaking techniques for beginning teachers.
3. To present a variety of techniques for the accomplished conductor.
4. To encourage teachers to use choral speaking in the development of oral communications skills.
5. To show that within the framework of choral speaking methodology and techniques, many variations and adaptations are possible.
6. To help develop creative approaches to the teaching of choral speaking.

Some of the values of choral speaking for young people are:

1. To provide a means of oral communication in a group setting.

Introduction

2. To enjoy group oral language participation.
3. To develop freedom of expression and communication.
4. To develop standard speech patterns and an awareness of the rhythmical structure of language.
5. To develop a fund of memorized poetry and prose.
6. To develop powers of discrimination and taste in literature.
7. To develop skills in listening to others.
8. To develop creative interpretative oral language skills.

Footnotes

[1] Shakespeare, *Hamlet,* act III, scene I.

[2] Hicks, Helen Gertrude, *The Reading Chorus* (New York: Noble and Noble Publishers, Inc., 1939), p. 2.

Chapter II

BACKGROUNDS OF CHORAL SPEAKING

The historical backgrounds of choral speaking stem from antiquity when groups chanted during religious ceremonies or rituals to invoke favour or appeasement from the wrath of unseen forces, or to lend voices in thanks for victories over enemies or for times of plenty. De Banke stated that:

> Many of the ancient forms of choral ceremonial are known to us not only by traces in still extant material once used for such purposes, but by some actual survivals among isolated peoples today. The five most prominent uses for choral ritual seem to have been — to praise, propitiate and supplicate the deity, to incite warriors to unrelenting slaughter, to celebrate victory in battle, to taunt the vanquished, and to lament the dead. The earliest recorded forms of the first are in the penitential psalms of the Chaldeans and the mantras of the Vedas. The same type is to be found in the litany used today in the Episcopal Church. The second can still be heard among the American Indians, the tribes of the Pacific Archipelagoes, and the natives of South Africa (they are in most cases performances of ritual for their own sake and have no present application). There is no older or more perfect example to illustrate the third use than the Song of Deborah, and until very recent times the poets have used their art to further vaingloriousness and the pomp and pride of so-called victory. Taunting songs are still chanted by the women of Arabian tribes, and Indian braves of the Southwest direct their taunts not against the vanquished but against the bachelors of the tribe. The last use reaches superb heights in the dithyramb and Greek tragedy, both of which had their origin in simple ritualistic lament for a dead hero, later identified with Dionysus. The profound lament of David for Saul and Jonathan is perhaps the most perfect example of ritualistic lament. There is fundamental quality about all elegiac forms, and it is not surprising to find such ancient communal chants among the peasantry and primitive peoples the world over. A remarkable survival is found in

Syria, where the rites and songs of mourning performed by women today bear a startling resemblance to those seen and heard by Jeremiah twenty-five centuries ago.

Hebrew religious literature has many evidences of voices speaking together. Ritual chanting in synagogues has long been part of services.[2] The psalms, developed with antiphonal parallelism of thought, though usually sung, may be spoken by groups of voices in apposition, as in many Protestant services today. The "Song of Deborah" in Judges V has refrain-like exclamations which would lend themselves to speech or singing choral responses:

> Bless the Eternal
> Bless the Eternal's power, my soul![3]

David's wonderful requiem in 2 Samuel 1:19-27 composed after the death of Saul and Jonathan in the battle with the Phillistines has a recurring refrain, "How are the mighty fallen."[4]

Evidence of choral chanting can be traced from ancient times. In times of bereavement:

> professional mourners usually women, ... hastened to the house with loud lamentations, weepings, wailings, music, and the singing of dirges interspersed with many an "Alas!" Sometimes both men and women joined in chanting memorial requiems especially for princely people.[5]

Although the laments were traditionally sung, the effect was that of the spoken voice chanting.

> From the time of Ezra on through many centuries the book of Lamentations had a specified time for its public reading or cantillation. The date was the ninth of Ab, late in the summer. The complete book was chanted, both morning and evening of this day.[6]

It was in Greek drama that choral speaking reached its highest historical plane.

> Five hundred years before Christ, Greek drama in its first stages consisted of choral odes recited or chanted with rhythmic bodily movements, honoring the god of the vintage, Dionysus. Later, soloists or individual speakers were added but ever the chorus played an important part. In the days of the

dramatist Aeschylus, about 500 B.C., when two soloists spoke the parts of several characters, a chorus of fifty maidens in the play "The Suppliants" was still the chief actor. Some portions of the play called for part speaking, and some for antiphonal speaking.[7]

The Greek choruses for the most part accomplished four things: (1) They related the details of tragedy too terrible to show on the stage; (2) pronounced philosophic interpretations of the deeds committed by the high born; (3) moralized over cause and effect; or (4) uttered the reactions of the people to the events on which they looked.[8]

However, the importance of choral speaking in drama diminished gradually.

...in the tragedies of Sophocles the chorus became subordinate to the dialogue, and in the tragedies of Euriphides the connection between chorus and action of the plays is often slight. When, in the Roman theater, the chorus was banished from the orchestra and given a place on the stage, its original purpose was lost and we find the numbers dwindling until only a remnant remains. In Senecan tragedy the chorus, reduced to seven in number, wanders on and off the stage during the action and finally appears only to supply the interlude between the acts.[9]

The Elizabethan dramatists employed a single character for the recitation of prologue or epilogue. In Henry V, one man is the chorus. In Milton's *Samson Agonistes* there appears to be vestiges of choral speaking in the chorus, but by the close of the sixteenth century the art of choral speaking in plays seems to have been lost.

In the days of the troubadours and minstrels choral speaking, as well as group singing, was a part of the life of rich and poor in Europe as refrains and verses were sung or chanted in response to the traveling bard's tales.

There is abundant evidence of the importance of the calling of jongleur or minstrel from the faint dawn of civilization in Europe down to, say, the sixteenth century...[10]

One of the most interesting forms was the tenson, "a lyrical dialogue between two people who discussed some point of amorous casuistry or matters of a religious, metaphysical or satirical nature."[11]

Impromptu verses and choruses and ballads were an accepted part of the social living and were "as much a folk activity as folk songs and folk tales."[1 2]

The most continuing historical line of choral speaking has been in the plainsong, or Gregorian chant, "Which grew up during the first centuries of Christianity, influenced possibly by the music of the Jewish synagogue and certainly the Greek modal system."[1 3] The plainsong is essentially a musical chant of religious liturgy.

> The simpler plainsong springs, one may suppose, from the natural tendency of the reader or speaker (especially in a large building) to utter his words on one note, with some dropping of the voice at the ends of sentences or verses. Plainsong rhythm is the free rhythm of speech, *i.e.* the beat falls irregularly, not as in poetry; it is a prose rhythm, which of course arises from the unmetrical character of the words to be recited — psalms, prayers, and the like.[14]

Congregational responses have remained an integral part of the liturgy of the English and Catholic church services, and in the new Catholic recitations of the mass in English there is evidence of a complete reliance upon choral speaking for the major section of the services, as the Introit, Gradual, Creed, and other sections are recited in unison by the audience.

In Protestant churches antiphonal reading of Biblical passages is a part of many services. The use of choral response in church services has been the most continuing link through the centuries in choral speaking.

Except for congregational responses in church services, the art of choral speaking received little emphasis from the time of the Elizabethan dramatists until the present day. Choral group speaking was supplanted by singing choirs, and the great surge of musical composition in the western world from 1600 onward gave little attention to group speaking. Individual oratory, individual voices in plays were, the media in the theater, and choral singing the media in the church.

About 1920 there was a general revival of choral speaking in Great Britain. This preceded in 1903 by Thomas Hardy's epic drama "The Dynasts," which contained choral passages comparable to Greek tragedy. In 1907 Dr. Bottomley experimented with verse speaking in unison speech in "The Riding to Lithuend." In 1922 the annual Verse Speaking Festival was begun at Oxford by John Masefield. In 1923 the Glasgow Verse Speaking Choir was organized. In these efforts Miss Marjorie Gullan was a prominent leader, and her books exemplify the ideas of this early movement.

During the next two decades many books were written, and choral speaking became an established part of the language arts programs of American elementary schools. Few books relating to methodology in choral speaking were written after 1945 but numerous anthologies of selections suitable for choral speaking were published.

Choral speaking has not yet gained a firm foothold in junior or senior high language classes or in church youth groups or adult organizations. At the present time, choral speaking seems to be a firmly established practice of the elementary school language arts program.

Footnotes

[1] De Banke, Cecile, *The Art of Choral Speaking* (Boston, Mass.: Baker's Plays, 1937), p. 18.

[2] Scholes, Percy A., *The Oxford Companion to Music* (New York: Oxford University Press, 1950), p. 483.

[3] Bible. Judges 5:9,21.

[4] *Ibid.* 2 Samuel 1:19-27.

[5] Grauman, Helen G., *Music in my Bible* (Mountain View, California: Pacific Press Publishing Association, 1956), p. 109.

[6] *Ibid.,* p. 109.

[7] Keppie, Elizabeth Evangeline, *The Teaching of Choric Speech* (Boston, Mass.: Expression Company, 1952), p. 9.

[8] Hicks, Helen Gertrude, *The Reading Chorus* (New York: Noble and Noble Publishers, Inc., 1939), p. 1.

[9] De Banke, Cecile, op. cit., p. 16.

[10] Scholes, op. cit., p. 580.

[11] Encyclopedia Britannica, 1965, th. ed., s.v. "Troubadours."

[12] Hicks, op. cit., p. 3.

[13] Scholes, op. cit., p. 737.

[14] *Ibid.,* p. 736.

Chapter III

THE PIED PIPER

> *For he led us, he said, to a joyous land,*
> *Joining the town and just at hand,*
> *Where waters gushed and fruit trees grew,*
> *And flowers put forth a fairer hue,*
> *And everything was strange and new.*
> *The sparrows were brighter than peacocks here,*
> *And their dogs outran our fallow deer,*
> *And honey-bees had lost their stings;*
> *And horses were born with eagle's wings:*
>
> The Pied Piper by Robert Browning[1]

Once upon a time, so the legend tells us, there was a Piper with a magic pipe and magic tune, and he piped the children away from their parents and homes to a land adults could not understand, to a land that only children knew — a special land where dreams and wishes come true.

Once upon a day there was also a teacher who was inspired by this tale, and she found a special set of pipes and learned how to play such wonderful tunes and ditties and enchanting tales that the children in her classroom left their play, their work, and followed her into the wonderful land where dreams come true — a land children know and understand; a land a few privileged teachers also know and understand.

What can the average teacher do to help her pupils enter the magic land? We know choral speaking will help; but if we announce to our pupils, "Today we are going to have choral speaking," the results are likely to be negligible. Love of poetry and beautiful prose develops slowly through listening, speaking, and reading.

It is unwise to plunge into choral speaking for choral speaking's sake and hope our children will become lovers of poetry and prose. We, as teachers, need to live and breathe and feel and above all love the beauties of our mother tongue and the beauties of our language. The lyrical poetry, the stirring speeches should be part and parcel of our speaking vocabularies. In essence, we should become vehicles for the interpretation of the poets.

Many teachers feel the mechanics and skills of good choral speaking are too difficult to master; but all teachers can become Pied Pipers and lead their pupils into the enchanted land of spoken poetry and prose.

Poetry is meant for reading aloud. It is best when shared with others. What would a simple nursery rhyme such as "Jack and Jill" mean to you if you had read it silently? It is the joy of speaking, and the pleasure of listening to the lilt of "went up the Hill," "AND <u>Jack</u> fell <u>down</u>" that makes the words live in memory.

> If children are to develop a genuine liking for poetry, they must hear quantities of it read aloud from their earliest years, and simultaneously begin to speak of it, and, later, read it aloud for themselves.[2]

At any grade level, whether it be primary or high school, pupils need to hear poetry if they are to understand and thrill to meanings and word patterns. Poetry reading time should be a happy time as pupils and teachers relax and enjoy living thoughts and living language. The teacher, as a reader, need not be a skilled orator, but she must be able to interpret the feelings, mood, and unique music of the particular poem as she sees and feels it.

What poetry should the teacher read? It is best to choose, not from prescribed lists, but from the poetry that means something special to you and read it as if it really were special, you will find that miraculously you have turned into a Pied Piper, and your pupils are leaving their work and their play to follow the magic of your soul as you reveal the touchstones of your feelings through your reading. Try it, and you will experience some of the happiest moments of your career, and these moments will become precious memories to your pupils. In truth, this is "the stuff" of which teaching is made.

Poetry with a flair of nonsense and a musical lilt will capture the children's interest. The ludicrousness of an OWL and a PUSSY CAT going to SEA in a PEA GREEN boat with HONEY and MONEY plus the wonderful chorus:

The Owl and the Pussy Cat
by Edward Lear [3]

O lovely pussy, O pussy, my love,
What a beautiful pussy you are,

You are
You are!

will capture the wee listener's ear as well as his funny bone.

The Mother Goose rhyme, To Market To Market, has a jiggedy rhythm that generations of children have enjoyed:

To Market To Market [4]

To market, to market, to buy a fat pig,
Home again, home again, jiggety jig.

To market, to market, to buy a fat hog,
Home again, home again, joggety jog.

To market, to market, to buy a plum bun,
Home again, home again, market is done.

Children are charmed by a ludicrous pig and the wonderful sound of many "n's" in Rose Fyleman's delightful "Mary Middling," and which should be read with verve and laughter.

Mary Middling
by Rose Fyleman [5]

Mary Middling had a pig,
Not very little and not very big,
Not very pink, not very green,
Not very dirty, not very clean,
Not very good, not very naughty,
Not very humble, not very haughty,
Not very thin, not very fat,
Now what would you give for a pig like that?

Intermediate grade children love Jonathan Bing, who seems to have more social troubles than they do, and to think he is going to VISIT THE KING! Every child knows deep inside himself that he is wiser than poor old Jonathan Bing, but sympathizes with him because they know how society frowns upon social *faux pas*, because their sensitive selves seem to commit a constant array of these.[6]

Preteens who long to live in the Pied Piper's world of strange language that only they understand will enjoy: Jabberwocky by Lewis Carrol.

Jabberwocky
by Lewis Carroll[7]

Twas brillig and the slithy toves
Did gyre and gimble in the wabe
All mimsy were the borogoves,
And the mome raths outgrabe.

Children who have memorized Hiawatha and know its rhythms and structure will find "The Modern Hiawatha" disconcerting and amusing, and they finally will try parodies of their own.

The Modern Hiawatha
by George A. Strong[8]

He killed the noble Mudjokovis
With the skin he made him mittens
Made them with the fur side inside,
Made them with the skin side outside,
He, to get the warm side inside,
Put the inside skin side outside.
He to get the cold side outside
Put the warm side fur side inside;
That's why he put the fur side inside,
Why he put the skin side outside,
Why he turned them inside outside!

Nonsense rhymes and strong rhythms will capture children's interests in poetry, and they will want the selections read over and

The Pied Piper

over again. Poems of mood may be brought into pupil repertoire gradually. Story poems of happy moments will capture fancies. Pupils will begin to develop perceptive powers of imagery as they read poems like "The Sandpiper." Do you see the wind-swept beach? Do you see a lonely child? Do you see a happy child? Have you ever had a happy moment like this one?

The Sandpiper
by Celia Thaxter[9]

Across the narrow beach we flit,
One little sandpiper and I,
And fast I gather, bit by bit,
The scattered driftwood bleached and dry,
The wild waves reach their hands for it,
The wild wind raves, the tide runs high,
As up and down the beach we flit, —
One little sandpiper and I.

Long narrative poems will cause some disinterested pupils to be carried away by the sheer excitement of the plot. What will the Dutch lad do when he hears the "trickling sound"? Will he run? What would you do if you were he?

The Leak in the Dike
by Phoebe Cary[10]

But hark! through the noise of waters
Comes a low, clear, trickling sound;
And the child's face pales with terror
And his blossoms drop to the ground!

Many a boy will thrill to a lad of yesteryear as you read **"Lincoln"** by Nancy Byrd Turner.[11]

There was a boy of other days
A quiet, awkward, earnest lad,
Who trudged long weary miles to get
A book on which his heart was set —
And then no candle had!

Teen-agers may be lured to the enchanted land of poetry and prose. The story of dauntless courage in the face of obvious defeat of the crew of "The Revenge" will thrill even the most blasé teen-ager, and he will realize that poetry is not necessarily sissy or feminine.

excerpts from **The Revenge**
by Alfred Lord Tennyson[12]

The little Revenge ran on
sheer into the heart of the foe,
With her hundred fighters on
deck, and her ninety sick below —
. . .
Thousands of their soldiers looked down from their
decks and laughed,
Thousands of their seamen made mock at the mad little craft
Running on and on, . . .

Ballads old and new have fascinated listeners down through the ages. Teens usually enjoy the happier ballads such as

"Get up and Bar the Door"[13]

They made a paction tween them twa,
They made it firm and sure,
That the first word whaer shoud speak,
Shoud rise and bar the door.

Sir Walter Scott's appeal is timeless for young people, containing as it does both romance and valour.

Lochinvar
by Sir Walter Scott[14]

O, young Lochinvar is come out of the west,
Through all the wide Border his steed was the best;
And save his good broadsword, he weapons had none,
He rode all unarmed, and he rode all alone.
So faithful in love, and so dauntless in war,
There never was a knight like the young Lochinvar.
. . . .

> There was racing and chasing, on Cannobie Lee,
> But the lost bride of Netherby ne'er did they see.
> So daring in love, and so dauntless in war.
> Have ye e'er heard of gallant like young Lochinvar?

After students have heard much poetry and prose read aloud, they will want to read and create for themselves. Choral speaking is one of the natural outcomes of these desires. One child or a group of children will wish to repeat a selection, and choral speaking will grow out of the needs of the class for a form of oral expression in which all may participate. Choral speaking should be considered as only part of the total program of language development. It will grow and flourish only in a reading-listening setting where the finest in literature and prose is presented in many ways. In the reading-listening setting children will gladly follow the teacher into the enchanted world of literature because the teacher is no longer a teacher but a Pied Piper with magic in her soul.

Footnotes

[1] Browning, Robert, "The Pied Piper of Hamlin," from the *Anthology of Children's Literature,* Ed. May Hill Arbuthnot (Chicago: Scott Foresman and Co., 1961), p. 27.

[2] Arbuthnot, Mae Hill, *Anthology of Children's Literature,* (Chicago: Scott Foresman and Co., 1961), p. lxiii.

[3] Lear, Edward, "The Owl and the Pussy Cat," from *Snug Under the Silver Umbrella,* Ed. Association for Childhood Education. Literature Committee. (New York: Macmillan Company, 1958).

[4] Mother Goose, "To Market To Market."

[5] Fyleman, Rose, "Mary Middling," from *Snug Under the Silver Umbrella,* p. 3.

[6] Brown, Beatrice Curtis, "Jonathan Bing," from *Favorite Poems Old and New,* Ed. Helen Ferris (Garden City, New York: Doubleday and Co., Inc., 1957), p. 335.

[7] Carroll, Lewis, "Jabberwocky," from *Favorite Poems Old and New,* p. 334.

[8] Strong, George A. "The Modern Hiawatha," from *Favorite Poems Old and New,* p. 337.

[9] Thaxter, Celia, "The Sandpiper," from *Favorite Poems Old and New,* p. 292.

[10] Cary, Phoebe, "The Leak in the Dike," from *Favorite Poems Old and New,* p. 556.

[11] Turner, Nancy Byrd, "Lincoln," from *Favorite Poems Old and New,* p. 439.

[12] Tennyson, Alfred Lord, "The Revenge in the Charge of the Light Brigade," from *Favorite Poems Old and New,* p. 564.

[13] "Get Up and Bar the Door," Old Ballad, from the *Arbuthnot Anthology*, p. 17.

[14] Scott, Sir Walter, "Lochinvar," from *The Poetical Works of Sir Walter Scott*, Ed. J. Logie Robertson (London: Oxford University Press, 1964), p. 142.

Chapter IV

METRICAL EMPHASIS IN CHORAL SPEAKING

There are two distinct schools of thought about the amount of emphasis that should be placed upon the metrical rhythmic structure of poetic works. One school believes that the metrical base of the poem should play an intrinsic part in oral interpretation, while the second believes that the interpretation of mood and meaning should determine the amount of emphasis placed upon the metrical base of the poem. Around these two ideas have developed methods of teaching, interpretation, and conducting.

The problem is compounded by a number of issues:

1. If children are taught to interpret poetry in a completely metrical fashion, they tend to develop sing-song meaningless interpretations.
2. If they are allowed to interpret freely, they may lose sight of the metrical quality inherent within poetry.
3. Most poets who have recorded metrically designed verse interpret orally with a definite metric structure.[1] Teachers who have heard these poets or their recordings[2] realize that this type of interpretation is not child-like and would have little appeal in the classroom, especially for young children.
4. Conducting techniques and attitudes of interpretation for both methods are essentially different.

Let us examine the two approaches as usually interpreted by classroom teachers. **Method I** will be used to designate the metrically-based technique in which rhythm is constantly present. **Method II** will designate the method in which the interpretation will determine the amount, if any, of stress upon the metrical poetic base.

Accents

In **Method I** some accent is placed upon each foot in the metrical line. This may be slight or emphasized, depending upon the particular interpretation. In "The Old Log House" by James S. Tippett, the emphasis in speaking would fall on the accented syllables of the two-foot line.

The Old Log House
by James S. Tippett[3]

	Number of accents per line
1. On a líttle knóll	2
2. At the édge of the wóod	2
3. My gréat great grándmother's	2
4. Fírst house stóod.	2

In **Method II** any number of interpretations of accent would be possible, whereas in **Method I** only one interpretation or a variation of the one method of accenting is possible. In **Method II** some groups might wish to accent as in **Method I** or some groups would interpret the four lines as prose. In one such interpretation lines 1, 2, and 3, 4 would constitute two phrases with a slight pause at the end of line 2 to show the rhythmic base:

1. On a little knoll 2. At the edge of the wood PAUSE
3. My great great grandmother's 4. First house stood

Conducting Techniques

In **Method I** "The Old Log House" definite vertical conducting movements would be used.*

1. On a little knoll

2. At the edge of the wood

*See chapter VIII for methods of conducting.

3. My gre̍at great grandmo̍ther's

4. Fi̍rst house sto̍od.

The arrows indicate downward beat or "one" beat of one-two conducting movement.

In order for all pupils to say words in unison it has come to be accepted that the teacher will "mouth" the words and the students will say the words precisely in time with the conductor's lip movements.

In **Method II** conducting movements would vary according to group interpretation. The conducting movements for the interpretation previously mentioned would be:

1. On a little knoll ─────────────────►
2. At the edge of the wood   HOLD ◄─────
3. My great great grandmother's ─────────►
4. First house stood. ◄───────────────

In this interpretation the conducting movements show where phrases begin and end, and also indicate pauses.

In **Method II** "mouthing" is not utilized except for beginning and ending of phrases or sections. Emphasis is placed upon saying phrases in unison. The flow of oral language is stressed rather than the metrical base of the selection.

Tonal Coloring (the shadings of sound from light to dark to express "sound as color, made audible")[4]

Both methods utilize individualized interpretations of tonal coloring.

Pacing (The rate of speed at which selection is spoken)

In both methods pace is determined by interpretation.

Pauses (the absence of sound)

In **Method I** pauses are utilized only when a rest or pause is called for in the metrical structure. In **Method II** pauses are determined by the interpretation of the selection.

In the following stanza from "The Old Log House" there would be no pauses at line ends in **Method I**. In **Method II** one interpretation might consider lines 1 and 2 as a unit. A pause might be utilized at the end of line 3 to cause a change of idea between lines 3 and 4:

1. The house was of logs   2. My grandmother said
3. With one big room   PAUSE
4. And a lean-to-shed.   NEW IDEA

Essentially **Method I** has the underlying rhythmical structure ever-present, and **Method II** utilizes the metrical structure when mood and meaning would be enhanced thereby.

The basic problem is whether poetry should be spoken, in group situations, with emphasis upon the metrical base, or whether it should be allied to oral prose. Is there a correct way to approach the problem? To which school of thought should one belong?

All approaches have a place in the creative teacher's technique. Difficulties over methods should not arise. The method that will best fulfill the particular choral speaking activity should be utilized. The metrical approach should be used when it enhances meaning. If the poem is akin to spoken language, a non-metrical approach is probably better. Rasmussen stated that:

> Knowledge and feeling must govern the amount of rhythm we put into a poem as we say it, but we must retain enough of the rhythmic pattern to create the mood the poet intended; at the same time we must cut through the meter enough to carry the finer shades of meaning and thought.[5]

When pre-planning a selection, read it metrically and non-metrically and listen for the strengths of each method. It is only by hearing a poem and listening carefully to the rhythmic structure that the value of metrical pauses and rhythms can be appreciated.

In "Mrs. Peck-Pigeon" by Eleanor Farjeon, the underlying pattern upon which the poem is based is a two-beat bobbing up and down of a pecking pigeon. Without this underlying rhythmic structure the word and sound pictures of a pecking bird are lost.

Mrs. Peck-Pigeon
by Eleanor Farjeon[6]

Mrs. Peck-Pigeon
Is picking for bread,
Bob-bob-bob
Goes her little round head.
Tame as a pussy cat
In the street
Step-step-step
Go her little red feet.
With her little red feet
And her little round head,
Mrs. Peck-Pigeon
Goes picking for bread.

The Old Log House
by James S. Tippett

On a little knoll
At the edge of the wood
My great-great-grandmother's
First house stood.

The house was of logs
My grandmother said
With one big room
And a lean-to-shed.

The logs were cut
And the house was raised
By pioneer men
In the olden days.

I like to hear
My grandmother tell
How they built the fireplace
And dug the well.

They split the shingles
They filled each chink
It's a house about which
I like to think.

Forever and ever
I wish I could
Live in a house
At the edge of a wood.

Footnotes

[1] Dolman, John, *The Art of Reading Aloud,* (New York: Harper and Brothers, 1956), p. 123.

[2] Refer to the Library of Congress, Music Department, for recordings of poems by poets.

[3] Tippett, James S., "The Old Log House," from *Favorite Poems Old and New,* p. 240.

[4] Rasmussen, Carrie, *Choral Speech for Speech Improvement* (Magnolis, Mass.: Expression Company, 1953), p. 36.

[5] Farjeon, Eleanor, "Mrs. Peck-Pigeon," from the *Arbuthnot Anthology,* p. 52.

[6] Welles, Winifred, "Behind the Waterfall," from the *Arbuthnot Anthology,* p. 149.

[7] Tippett, op. cit.

Chapter V

THE BEGINNING TEACHER

This chapter is written for the teacher who wishes to take the first steps toward proficiency in the art of choral speaking. What should one do? Where should one begin?

Here are some practical suggestions:

I. Look through your favorite poetry books and choose a few poems that appeal to you and which you believe will appeal to your pupils. Poems with strong rhythmical structure and with a sense of humour are easiest for the beginning teacher. Choose poems of universal appeal rather than those written to or about one individual. For each poem find out as much as possible about the poet and the reasons why he wrote the poem. Perhaps you will wish to find a number of pictures to illustrate ideas or new concepts found in the poem. However, you may wish the poem itself to convey word pictures of meanings so that each child can develop his own mental image.

II. Read the poem silently to yourself, endeavoring to feel the mood as deeply as possible. Read the poem aloud and try to express the thoughts as well as you can. Listen to your voice. Do the thoughts sound convincing? Do not sing-song the poem. Read as you would talk to a friend. Read as if the words and thoughts were your own and you were trying to convince your friend of your sincerity.

III. As you read, think of the big ideas. Think of the mood and tonal qualities. Try to realize points of intensity or conflicts within the poem. Use the dictionary to check pronunciations of words. If possible, hear your rendition on a tape recorder. Be critical of your own reading. Is your enunciation clear? Are the big ideas convincing? Have you captured the mood?

IV. Stand in front of a mirror and read the poem over. Do you look convincing? Is there a sparkle in your eyes as you read the poem?

V. As you read, try to develop simple hand movements that will enable your children to begin a selection together and maintain a steady, uniform rhythm. A simple, free, and easy beginning gesture is best.

If you have no previous experience in choral conducting, you may find the following ideas useful in beginning stages until you develop your own conducting patterns:

1. With arms bent and fingers cupped, place your hands in position A.

2. Move hands from A to B. This is the "Get-set" or "Get-ready" movement that precedes the first strong metrical beat of your poem.

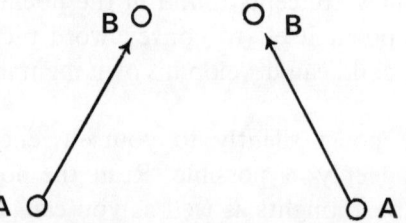

3. With a strong movement, move hands downward from B to C on first metrical beat of poem. Both hands or right hand alone may be used on downbeat.

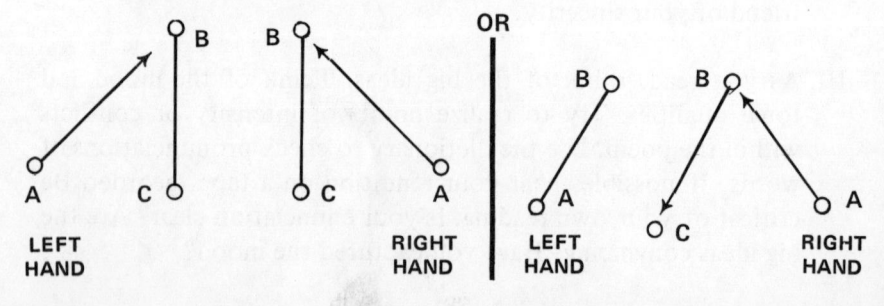

LEFT HAND   RIGHT HAND   OR   LEFT HAND   RIGHT HAND

As you move into strong downbeat stroke BC, say first word or words of poem. Practice the upward AB and downward BC movements a few times until you automatically say the first word on the downward sweep BC of your hands.

If you wish to convey the structure of the poem, repeat the poem and continue a rhythmic movement of the right arm. Conducting the complete poem is not necessary for beginning choral speech work, but you should conduct the first line so that everyone will begin together.

VI. Read poem and conduct while "mouthing" words soundlessly into a mirror. This will help you later when you do not wish your voice heard while conducting.

VII. Try to decide which sections of your poem would be best repeated by the complete choir — small groups, individuals, light voices, or dark voices. Write your ideas in the margin of your text.

VIII. Mark climax line.

IX. Say your poem again trying to abide by the pattern you have developed.

X. Now you are ready to meet your class.

Planning a Choral Speaking Lesson

Choral speaking lessons, as a rule, should be short. It is better to have three fifteen minute lessons spaced over two or three days than one thirty or forty-five minute lesson. Children will learn poems more quickly and retention will be greater if learning periods are short and placed at intervals.

Choral speech should be an integral part of classroom living along with music, art, and physical education activities. A lesson plan would not necessarily be carried out in its entirety at one time. It should be an ongoing plan spread over a period of time. A section of the plan could be presented between arithmetic and social studies classes in the morning; repeated while the students are preparing to go home at noon; and the remainder taught in the afternoon as a break in the midst of group reading sessions.

LESSON PLAN OUTLINE

I. Introduction
 1. Present backgrounds of poem — setting, poets, reason for writing.
 2. Recite selection to class setting mood and basic rhythmic structure.
 3. Clarify difficult meaning concepts by discussion and audio-visual aids.

II. Body of Lesson
This is based upon the learning pattern of
WHOLE-PART-WHOLE-PART

WHOLE
 1. Recite <u>selection</u> to class.
 2. Recite selection while class whispers as much as they remember.
 3. Recite selection while class speaks softly.
 4. Present introductory conducting beats. Explain motions to class.
 5. Place hands in position A. All children look at your hands, and at first movement of hands they take a breath. Show them how to breathe by expanding rib cage sideways and not lifting shoulders.

A 〇╱┃╲ A

PART
 6. Begin conducting movements and lead children with your voice as a guide to end of the <u>first</u> <u>thought</u> <u>idea</u>.
 7. Repeat 6 until children can start together.
 8. Say <u>complete</u> <u>selection</u> with conducting movements while children speak in soft voices. Your voice,

WHOLE	initially, must be heard slightly above children's to hear nuance patterns.
	9. Repeat <u>second</u> <u>thought</u> <u>section</u> of selection.
PART	10. Children repeat in normal tones while you speak and guide nuances.
	11. Children repeat while you "mouth" words and they try to keep pace with you by following your lip movements.
	12. If they falter, repeat 10, then 11, until they can copy your pattern.
	13. For each thought or idea section of poem repeat 9, 10, and 11. Intersperse these sectional learnings with 8 or with stanza repetitions. Follow the WHOLE-PART-WHOLE-PART-plan of learning.

After the mood and basic patterns of the selection have been established, the children need to learn to interpret poetic moods for themselves. Ask various students to interpret a thought orally and let class discuss which idea they believe presents the meaning most adequately.

Do not give a copy of the poem to your class before the mood and rhythm and a goodly portion of the memorizing has been done. The beauties of oral language are nullified when students stumble through oral reading. A choral speaking lesson is essentially a hearing-type lesson and not a reading lesson.

If pupils are good readers or if you wish to teach reading in conjunction with choral speech, use copy but teach as an oral reading lesson.

Some Do's for the Beginning Teacher

1. Know your selection well. Be able to recite it from memory.
2. Keep choral speech periods short.
3. Clarify all difficult concepts, words, or phrase meanings.
4. Smile and be happy. Be certain these are happy moments for children. Smiling faces produce light, bright tones. Sad faces produce heavy, dull tones.
5. Initially, present selection as a whole.
6. Intersperse sectional learnings with whole poem learnings.

7. Practise the initial entry to your conducting until children can do it automatically.
8. Keep voices light. Maintain a conversational tone. Avoid sing-song style of recitation.
9. Teach many poems. Build pupil's poetic repertory.
10. Afford pupils good examples of correct speech.
11. As soon as children can say selection reasonably well, do not recite poem with them. Teach them to listen to each other's voices and blend tones. Discourage any copying of adult tones, especially male voices.
12. Know the types of voices and range of vocal tone in your class. During oral reading lessons make notations of general voice types. In lower grades the range is narrow, and in upper grades the range widens. Try different arrangements of voices to utilize the range within your choir.
13. Try varying seating arrangements. In early stages it is easier to conduct if each vocal section sits together.

On the following pages three lesson plans are developed in detail. In the first, the teacher plans the exact way in which the selection should be interpreted and teaches this plan to pupils. This is useful when dealing with immature groups or groups with little oral speaking knowledge of literature. The second plan allows for some teacher direction, when needed, but relies upon pupil creativity for most of the oral interpretation. The third plan is pupil created and developed.

Each plan is a suggestion for a possible lesson. Each teacher must create her own ways of helping pupils enjoy and learn oral interpretative skills.

LESSON PLAN I — A Teacher-directed Lesson

— to be used with groups who need much help in memorization skills, understanding of concepts, and oral interpretation of poetry.

THE LULLABY OF THE IROQUOIS

Grade level — 3

I. Materials Used
   1. Johnson, Pauline. *Flint and Feather.*[1]

2. Recording of Iroquois dance or war song.
3. Map of Iroquois area.
4. Pictures of heron, plover, night owl, oak tree with Indian cradle hanging on a branch.
5. Indian cradle with a doll.
6. Pictures of Iroquois Indian in war dress.

II. General Purposes Lesson
   1. To help students gain an insight into the home lives of Indian peoples.
   2. To help pupils understand that Iroquois fathers and mothers loved their children and expressed this love through kindness and care.
   3. To help pupils appreciate and love the beauty of the American countryside as did the Iroquois.

III. Specific Purposes of Lesson
   1. To add the poem to the children's memory bank of poetry.
   2. To discover how Indian children were rocked to sleep in a special kind of cradle.
   3. To enjoy the lilt of the lullaby rhythm.
   4. To learn about the wild life depicted in the poem (heron, plover, night owl).
   5. To understand the meaning of the following phrases in the poem:
      haunt on the hill
      shielding their sleep
      unyielding to sleep

IV. Choral Speaking Pattern
    Unison voices speaking softly in lullaby rhythm.

V. Introduction
   As you listen to a few moments of this recording, decide which group of American people are making the sounds you hear. (Play record.)
   What peoples do you hear? What are some of the tribes of Indians you know about? Here is a map of the Great Lakes region showing where some tribes live. What are some of the tribal names on the map? In what areas of the Great Lakes

region did they live? What is the general name given to all these tribes?

Show picture of Iroquois warrior.

The Iroquois warriors were noted for their bravery, but all was not war. Do you suppose Iroquois braves loved their homes and wives and children very much? Where did the warriors' families live? What was a baby called? Where did the papoose sleep?

Show cradle and let children talk about construction. Where could the papoose be hung to rock it to sleep?

Listen to this lullaby and find out where this Indian baby slept.

Read poem placing pictures on bulletin board or flannel board as poem is repeated (heron, plover, night owl, oak tree, camp fire, curling grey smoke, papoose in a cradle).

Where did the papoose sleep? Was it a good place to sleep? Why didn't the baby go to sleep? What does the mother call her baby? Why does she call it a brown baby bird?

As I recite the poem to you again, close your eyes and see if in your mind you can picture all the things the baby saw from its cradle.

VI. Body of Lesson

Lullaby of the Iroquois
by Pauline Johnson

1. Little brown baby-bird, lapped in your nest,
2. Wrapped in your nest,
3. Strapped in your nest.
4. Your straight little cradle-board rocks you to rest;
5. Its hands are your nest;
6. Its bands are your nest;
7. It swings from the down-bending branch of the oak.
8. You watch the camp flame, and the curling grey smoke;
9. But, oh, for your pretty black eyes sleep is best, –
10. Little brown baby of mine, go to rest.

11. Little brown baby-bird swinging to sleep,
12. Winging to sleep,
13. Singing to sleep,
14. Your wonder-black eyes that so wide open keep,
15. Shielding their sleep,

16. Unyielding to sleep,
17. The heron is homing, the plover is still,
18. The night-owl calls from his haunt on the hill,
19. Afar the fox barks, afar the stars peep, —
20. Little brown baby of mine, go to sleep.

1. As I say the first verse, repeat it softly with me. Lines 1, 2, 3.
2. Repeat the three words that tell how the baby-bird was held in the nest. What do they mean?
3. Class repeats lines 1, 2, 3.
4. Teacher recites lines 4, 5, 6.
5. Class repeats 4, 5, 6.
6. What are the hands? What are the bands? Why is the oak branch bent?
7. Teacher recites line 7.
8. Class repeats.
9. Teacher recites line 8.
10. Class repeats.
11. Teacher says lines 9, 10.
12. Class repeats softly.
13. In the second verse listen to the words that show the gentle rocking of the cradle in the wind.
    Teacher recites second verse emphasizing all "ing" words.
    Children repeat as well as they can.
14. Let's repeat the rocking words. Teacher says phrase and children repeat. Children do not say phrases with her.
    They learn to listen and copy her pattern.
     swinging to sleep
     winging to sleep
     singing to sleep
     shielding their sleep
     unyielding to sleep
15. Go back to verse one to reinforce learning before it is forgotten. This time the teacher conducts entry and practises first line until children begin in accord with hand movements, not with teacher's voice.

    Upswing AB is preparatory and pupils recite word "little" on downswing BC.

A ⭯ B C

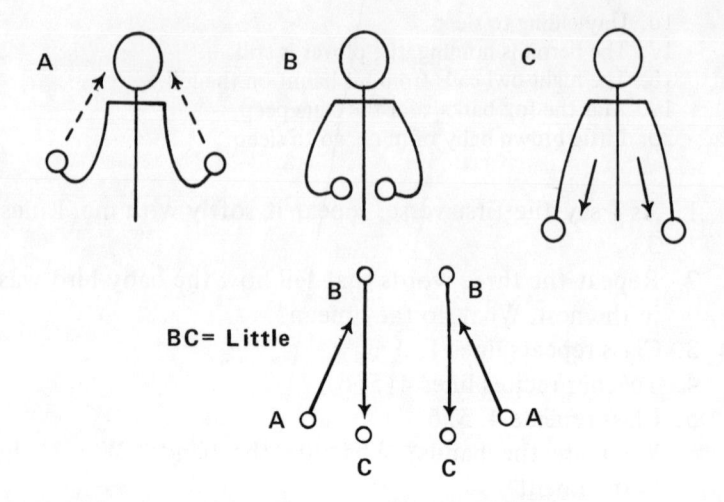

BC = Little

16. Teacher recites lines 1, 2, 3. Children repeat.
17. Teacher recites lines 1, 2, 3. Children repeat.
18. Teacher recites line 4.
19. Children recite lines 1, 2, 3, 4.
20. Teacher recites lines 5, 6. Children repeat.
21. Children repeat lines 1-6.
22. Teacher recites lines 5, 6, 7. Children repeat. (While children are repeating, the teacher does not conduct or speak unless pupils have difficulty.)
23. Teacher recites line 8. Children repeat.
24. Teacher recites lines 5, 6, 7, 8. Children repeat.
25. Children repeat lines 1-8.
26. Teacher recites lines 9, 10. Children repeat 9, 10.
27. Children repeat verse while teacher conducts and "mouths" words to help children keep together when they do not have teacher's immediately repeated pattern to copy.
28. In the second verse what were the rocking words we learned? Teacher repeats lines 14, 15, 16. Why were the baby's eyes shielding sleep? What does shield mean? Why were they unyielding to sleep? Discuss. (Activity: Dictionary meanings of these two words.) What other words could Miss Johnson have used? Why did she use shielding and unyielding?
29. Teacher repeats lines 11-16. (Note: After the previous reinforcements these lines should be learned easily.)

The Beginning Teacher 39

30. Teacher repeats lines 17, 18. Children repeat.
31. Why is the heron homing? Where is the night owl?
32. Children and teacher together say lines 11-18.
33. Teacher recites 19, 20. Children repeat.
34. Teacher and children say 19, 20 together.
35. Teacher and children repeat 11-20 together. This is done to help children feel the depths of mood that can be conveyed by the teacher's voice.
36. Children repeat complete poem while teacher conducts, and if necessary to hold group together, "mouths" words while children follow.
   Any section of the poem they do not know should be reviewed.

VII. Other Activities

At this point in the learning process the children understand meanings of the poem, have words memorized, and know basic nuance patterns as depicted by the teacher.

Some suggestions for polishing enunciation of the poem are:
1. Work on beautiful, unified enunciation in the "ped" sound in lapped, wrapped, strapped. Be certain that they all say it together and you can hear all voices saying it exactly in unison.
2. "in" and "your" should be clear.
3. Listen for the "n" and "s" sounds in "bands."
4. Listen for the "t" in "nest."
5. Listen for the "h" in "heron," in "homing," and "haunt on the hill."
6. Listen for all the "ing" sounds in verse 2.

Have different children repeat lines 4, 7, 8, 14, 18, 19 and try to develop thought, meaning, and word pictures. Let class copy the child's rendition that appeals most to them and incorporate this into the way poem is said.

Recite poem while children slowly rock back and forth in a very slow rocking motion of one beat to lines 1 and 2 and two beats to line 3.

Each thought idea in the poem could be depicted by children in picture form; and as the poem is recited, the joined pictures which they have made could be unrolled on a roll-type children's movie.

The class might like to experiment with the effects of this poem said in parts and with single voices, but the writer believes the poem tends to lend itself better to unison voices softly speaking in a lullaby rhythm.

LESSON PLAN II — Some Teacher direction

— pupils create most of ideas with some help from the teacher.

Note differences between this plan and Lesson I: a teacher-directed lesson. This plan is a suggestion to be used when pupils begin to create oral moods and interpret poetry themselves.

JOHATHAN BING

Grade level — 5

I. Materials Used
  1. "Jonathan Bing Visits the King" by Beatrice Curtis Brown[2]
     No visual materials are used because it is purposed to help pupils develop their own mental images of the story.

II. General Purposes of Lesson
  1. To have fun with poetry.
  2. To gain some insight into the literature of nonsense verse.

III. Specific Purposes of Lesson
  1. To enjoy Jonathan's predicament.
  2. To develop individual ways of expressing the dialogue of poem.
  3. To develop mental pictures of words, scenes, and characters.
  4. To encourage students to read other nonsense verse.
  5. To encourage students to write nonsense verse.

IV. Choral Speaking Pattern
  In this lesson, patterns will be developed with children. The teacher will not impose her patterns on the selection unless students need ideas.

Four-beat rhythm. Some lines have 3 beats and one rest.

V. Introduction

```
??????????????????????????????????
?           Jonathan Bing         ?
??????????????????????????????????
```

On this card is placed the name of the person about whom Beatrice Curtis Brown wrote a funny poem. Why do you suppose we have surrounded his name with question marks?

As the poem is read, try to decide what Jonathan Bing was really like. Where did he live? What did he do for a living? Who were the people he met? What did they look like? What did Jonathan Bing look like? What were the houses and streets like? Would you like to live in Jonathan Bing's town?

(Questions may be placed on chalk board)
Read poem.
Discuss questions.

What is an Archbishop? Where does he live? Why would he know how Jonathan should dress when visiting the king?

Had Jonathan ever visited the king before? Why?

What did Jonathan's beautiful tie look like? Why do you suppose it was so difficult for Jonathan to get ready to see the king?

Give pupils copies of poem.
Read poem again conducting with four beats to a line.

```
    1     2       3          4
Poor old Jonathan Bing      (rest)
      1       2        3      4
Went out in his carriage to visit the King
```

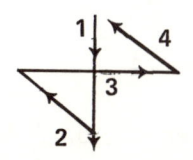

Observe the rests and have pupils read softly while you conduct and recite poem.
Have pupils watch you while you recite and conduct.
Let them count the four beats to a line.
Why do you think Beatrice Brown chose a four rhythm for this poem? Would another rhythm have been as useful?
Is there any reason for having the rests in the poem?

VI. Lesson

Jonathan Bing
by Beatrice Curtis Brown[12]

1. Poor old Jonathan Bing
2. Went out in his carriage to visit the King,
3. But everyone pointed and said, "Look at that!
4. Jonathan Bing has forgotten his hat!"
5. (He'd forgotten his hat!)

6. Poor old Jonathan Bing
7. Went home and put on a new hat for the King,
8. But up by the palace a soldier said, "Hi!
9. You can't see the King; you've forgotten your tie!"
10. (He'd forgotten his tie!)

11. Poor old Jonathan Bing
12. He put on a BEAUTIFUL tie for the King,
13. But when he arrived an Archbishop said, "Ho!
14. You can't come to court in pyjamas, you know!"

15. Poor old Jonathan Bing
16. Went home and addressed a short note to the King:
17. If you please will excuse me
18. I won't come to tea;
19. For home's the best place for
20. All people like me!

Ask four or five students to give their own interpretations of the following passages:
1. Line 3 last phrase and line 4.
2. Line 8 last word and line 9.
3. Line 13 last word and line 14.
4. Lines 17-20.
5. Lines 5 and 10 said after preceding phrase. Many variations can be developed depending upon interpretation of lines 4 and 9.

The class listens carefully as each student interprets the passage. Analyze each interpretation:
1. Does the speaker really mean what he is saying?
2. Do you think the speaker can see in his mind the scene he is depicting?
3. Is the speaker really playing the character role?
4. Which speakers are most convincing? Why?
5. Are there other possible interpretations?
6. Does the speaker convey to you the true meaning of the poem? If not, what do you think is needed? Demonstrate.

When pupils decide that one version of a line or phrase is what they believe most suitable, the child who developed it repeats it and the class copies the nuances and tone. The class may suggest variations on a particular interpretation, and many ideas may be developed.

The teacher should have many or several versions of interpretation prepared and be able to present ideas when the class needs guidance.

The teacher must tie suggestions into a unified whole:
1. What is the most important idea in each verse?
2. Where is the climax of ideas?
3. How should we interpret lines 1, 6, 11, and 15? What is their relationship to each other? to the poem as a whole?
4. Class repeats poem as a whole several times until all the separately developed parts become as one.

Practise initial conducting gestures as in first lesson plan in order to insure accurate attack on initial phrase.

At this point the pupils should have memorized the poem and have gained facility in individual interpretations.

VII. Other Activities
1. Write descriptive phrases of scenes and characters:
    Jonathan Bing: old and grizzled, quiet, kind and shy, confused.
    the town: winding, dusty streets, redtiled roofs, laughing faces of the shop-keepers.
2. Pupils make bulletin board displays of nonsense verse.
3. Pupils try to create nonsense verses or stories of their own.
4. Build a class booklet of nonsense verse and stories.

LESSON PLAN III – Pupil Created and Directed

AIRPLANE POEMS

Grade Level – 4

I. Materials Used
   1. McB. Green, Mary. "Aeroplane"[3]
   2. Meigs, Mildred Plew. "Silver Ships"[4]
   3. Tippett, James S. "Up in the Air"[5]
   4. Author Unknown. "Taking Off"[6]
   5. Frost, Frances M. "Night Plane"[7]

II. General Purpose of Lesson
   1. To help pupils choose poems for choral speaking.
   2. To give pupils the opportunity to create their own group interpretations of poetry.

III. The Lesson

This lesson would arise from the pupils' interest in airplanes which might be derived from a Social Studies unit about Transportation, or a Science unit about the principles of light.

As the pupils develop the particular unit, they will find stories and poems about airplanes and will wish to share these with the class. In a class where the basic elements of choral speaking have been taught, pupils will desire to share these chorally with each other.

The teacher might read "Silver Ships" by Cornelia Meigs and suggest that pupils bring in other poems to share with the class.

The pupils should be guided in their choice of poems for choral work. "Silver Ships" in the first person singular may or may not be a choice. However the ideas are universal, and pupils might wish to develop the poem chorally.

When the pupils have assembled a few poems, divide into groups and plan oral presentations. The groups should present poems to the class, and interpretations should be discussed. For pupils who are beginning this work, it is sometimes more valuable if all the groups work on the same poem at the same time in order to experience varied interpretations.

Encourage the pupils to try solo parts, pantomine actions, charades about well-known poems, musical backgrounds, flip charts of pictures they have drawn, and the writing of simple plays or poems using ideas from their poems.

These group choral activities will tend to be noisy and, if possible, activity areas outside the regular classroom will be needed.

The teacher, as a guide in these activities, must be prepared to:
1. Teach a group or the class when the need arises.
2. Have many ideas about each poem to present to groups when interest flags or the creative process bogs down.
3. Refrain from pushing teacher-designed ideas upon pupils.
4. Help pupils develop techniques whereby they can speak rhythmically together. The writer believes that much of the awkwardness and ineptness of pupil performances is solved if the teacher helps pupils begin a selection and also conducts the first part of the poem. Some pupils will become adept in these skills, but most student groups need some teacher direction.
5. Time group activities so that interest remains high. Several 15-20 minute classes are usually better than one long time block.
6. Plan group lessons. Love for poetry and choral speaking doesn't "just happen." Teacher planning brings it about.
7. Enjoy your choral speaking classes. Truly love the poetry you present and your pupils will be inspired.

IV. Suggestions for Teacher Notes

The teacher should have prepared suggestions for each poem. Some suggestions for the "Airplane" poems follow: (Remember, these are your ideas. Use them sparingly. Let the children be the creators.)

"Taking Off" Author Unknown
1. Two lines each may be read by 4 pupils.
2. One pupil reads 2 lines.
   At each succeeding 2 lines another pupil is added.
   All pupils read last 2 lines.
3. Each 2 lines may be illustrated by a simple picture.

"Up in the Air" James S. Tippett

1. Verse: Recite in unison.
   Chorus: Recite softly.
2. Verse: Group recite.
   Chorus: One voice.
3. The poem could be interpreted in creative dance.

"Aeroplane" Mary McB. Green

1. Humming could be used throughout the selection.
2. Divide group in 2 sections and recite lines alternately.
3. Utilize tape recorder to develop sound effects.

"Night Plane" France M. Frost

1. Use unison with one voice louder than others.
2. Write a play in which the midnight plane talks to people in villages, towns, and farms.

The remainder of Chapter V presents the poems cited in the exemplary units.

Lullaby of the Iroquois
by Pauline Johnson[9]

Little brown baby-bird, lapped in your nest,
Wrapped in your nest,
Strapped in your nest,
Your straight little cradle-board rocks you to rest;
Its hands are your nest;
Its bands are your nest;
It swings from the down-bending branch of the oak;
You watch the camp flame, and the curling gray smoke;
But, oh, for your pretty black eyes sleep is best, —
Little brown baby of mine, go to rest.

Little brown baby-bird swinging to sleep,
Winging to sleep,
Singing to sleep,
Your wonder-black eyes that so wide open keep,
Shielding their sleep,

Unyielding to sleep,
The heron is homing, the plover is still,
The night-owl calls from his haunt on the hill,
Afar the fox barks, after the stars peep, —
Little brown baby of mine, go to sleep.

Taking Off
Author Unknown[10]

The airplane taxis down the field
And heads into the breeze,
It lifts its wheels above the ground,
It skims above the trees,
It rises high and higher
Away up toward the sun,
It's just a speck against the sky
— And now it's gone.

Night Plane
by Frances M. Frost[11]

The midnight plane with its riding lights
looks like a footloose star
wandering west through the blue-black night
to where the mountains are,

a star that's journeyed nearer earth
to tell each quiet farm
and little town, "Put out your lights,
children of earth. Sleep warm."

Jonathan Bing
by Beatrice Curtis Brown[12]

Poor old Jonathan Bing
Went out in his carriage to visit the King,
But everyone pointed and said, "Look at that!
Jonathan Bing has forgotten his hat!"
(He'd forgotten his hat!)

Poor old Jonathan Bing
Went home and put on a new hat for the King,
But up by the palace a soldier said, "Hi!
You can't see the King; you've forgotten your tie!"
(He'd forgotten his tie!)

Poor old Jonathan Bing
He put on a BEAUTIFUL tie for the King,
But when he arrived an Archbishop said, "Ho!
You can't come to court in pyjamas, you know!"

Poor old Jonathan Bing
Went home and addressed a short note to the King:
If you please will excuse me
I won't come to tea;
For home's the best place for
All people like me!

Up in the Air
by James S. Tippett[13]

Zooming across the sky
Like a great bird you fly,
   Airplane,
   Silvery white
   In the light.

Turning and twisting in air,
When shall I ever be there,
   Airplane,
   Piloting you
   Far in the blue?

Aeroplane
by Mary McB. Green[14]

There's a humming in the sky
There's a shining in the sky
Silver wings are flashing by
Silver wings are shining by
Aeroplane
Aeroplane
Flying – high.

Silver wings are shining
As it goes gliding by
First it zooms
And it booms
Then it buzzes in the sky
Then its song is just a drumming
A soft little humming
Strumming
Strumming

The wings are very little things
The silver shine is gone
Just a little black speck
Away down the sky
With a soft little strumming
A far-away humming
Aeroplane
Aeroplane
Gone — by.

Silver Ships
by Mildred Plew Meigs[15]

There are trails that a lad may follow
    When the years of his boyhood slip,
But I shall soar like a swallow
    On the wings of a silver ship,

Guiding my bird of metal,
    One with her throbbing frame,
Floating down like a petal,
    Roaring up like a flame;

Winding the wind that scatters
    Smoke from the chimney's lip,
Tearing the clouds to tatters
    With the wings of a silver ship;

Grazing the broad blue sky light
    Up where the falcons fare,
Riding the realms of twilight,
    Brushed by a comet's hair;

Snug in my coat of leather,
    Watching the skyline swing,
Shedding the world like a feather
    From the tip of a tilted wing.

There are trails that a lad may travel
    When the years of his boyhood wane,
But I'll let a rainbow ravel
    Through the wings of my silver plane.

Footnotes

[1] Johnson, Pauline, "The Lullaby of the Iroquois," from *Flint and Feather* (Toronto: The Musson Book Co., Ltd., 1931), p. 96.

[2] Brown, Beatrice Curtis, "Jonathan Bing," from *Jonathan Bing and Other Verses* (New York: Oxford University Press, 1936), p. 132.

[3] Mc B. Green, Mary, "Aeroplane," from the *Arbuthnot Anthology*, p. 81.

[4] Meigs, Mildred Plew, "Silver Ships," from the *Arbuthnot Anthology*, p. 81.

[5] Tippett, James S., "Up in the Air," from the *Arbuthnot Anthology*, p. 81.

[6] Author Unknown, "Taking Off," from the *Arbuthnot Anthology*, p. 81.

[7] Frost, Frances M., "Night Plane," from the *Arbuthnot Anthology*, p. 82.

[8] Johnson, *op. cit.*, p. 96.

[9] Author Unknown, *op. cit.*, p. 81.

[10] Frost, *op. cit.*, p. 82.

[11] Brown, *op. cit.*, p. 132.

[12] Tippett, *op. cit.*, p. 81.

[13] McB. Green, *op. cit.*, p. 81.

[14] Meigs, *op. cit.*, p. 81.

Chapter VI

CHOICE OF CHORAL SPEAKING SELECTIONS

Of all the poetry and prose available for children some selections are for reading aloud, some for fun-time, some to listen to, some to be savored when one is alone, and some to use in choral work. A choral speaking selection may be chosen for its content, structure, appropriateness to pupil developmental level, or to meet the needs of a particular group of students. "... the final test, however, of Choral Speech as an artistic instrument must always be whether the poem gains by being voiced chorally ..."[1]

When choosing selections for content, these guidelines should be noted:

1. Choose selections with themes of universality of experience.
2. Selections with group consciousness or group emotions are more satisfactory than those dealing with individual feelings and moods. However, some individual poems with universality of experience may be used.
3. Choose selections with a social element in their origin such as ballads, sea-chanteys, or marching-type poems.
4. Humorous verse, because it can be shared with others, is ideal for all age groups.
5. Epic writing such as "John Brown's Body" by Stephen Vincent Benet is good material because of the breadth, depth, and scope of meaning and structure inherent within it.
6. Philosophical materials may have great impact in choral reading situations if the ideas presented have group appeal and are directed toward an audience. Vachel Lindsay's poem, "Abraham Lincoln Walks at Midnight" is an example of this type.
7. Choose selections which will enlarge pupil knowledge of moods, ideas, and structures of literary works.

When choosing poetry for choral speaking, the structure, in terms of speaking arrangements of the group, is a consideration. Some of the usual structures are as follows:

I. Unison

Most poems suitable for choral speaking may be spoken by a choir in unison. Although it is the most used form in choral speech arrangements in elementary schools, it is the most difficult to perform well:

> ... because a group of people must be unified in thought and feeling and voices must be artistically blended; in addition, they must have variety with control, flexibility with restraint. These things cannot be accomplished at once. A group of people must work together a long time to achieve this.[2]

II. Solo with Refrain

This type is reminiscent of the ballads sung and spoken by minstrels of long ago and is a popular form in the folk-song revival of today. Students of all ages enjoy this type especially if the class is grouped informally around a central speaker. Ballads, carols, marches, and poetry of folk-tale nature may be used.

III. Two-part work, Antiphonal and Dialogue

Some selections are structured as a balance between two voices or two groups of voices and are spoken antiphonally or in dialogue between two similar or contrasting types of voices. The Beatitudes[3] is structured antiphonally:

> Blessed are the poor in spirit: for theirs is the kingdom
>   of heaven.
> Blessed are they that mourn: for they shall be comforted.

IV. Line-a-child or Sequential

Each line is a thought unit and may be spoken by one child or a group of children sequentially:

Choice of Choral Speaking Selections

Pippa's Song
by Robert Browning[4]

Solo 1	The year's at the spring
Solo 2	And the day's at the morn:
Solo 3	Morning's at seven;
Solo 4	The hillside's dew pearled;
Solo 5	The lark's on the wing;
Solo 6	The snail's on the thorn;
Unison:	God's in his heaven —
	All's right with the world!

V. Part Speaking and Part Speaking Combined with Group Responses

Selections with diverse structures sometimes lend themselves to a combination of solo, group, and whole choir responses.

The Mysterious Cat
by Vachel Lindsay[5]

Sop.	I saw a proud mysterious cat,
2nd Sop.	I saw a proud mysterious cat,
Alto	Too proud to catch a mouse or rat —
Sop.	Mew, (2nd sop.) mew, (alto) mew.
Sop.	But catnip she would eat and purr
2nd Sop.	But catnip she would eat and purr
Alto	And goldfish she did much prefer —
Sop.	Mew, (2nd sop.) mew, (alto) mew.
Solo	I saw a cat (unison) 'twas but a dream
Solo	Who scorned the slave that brought her cream —
Sop.	Mew, (2nd sop.) mew, (alto) mew.
Sop.	Unless the slave were dressed in style,
2nd Sop.	Unless the slave were dressed in style,
Alto	And knelt before her all the while —
Sop.	Mew, (2nd sop.) mew, (alto) mew.
Sop.	Did you ever hear of a thing like that?
	(rapidly within the group)
2nd Sop.	Did you ever hear of a thing like that?
Alto	Did you ever hear of a thing like that?
Sop.	Oh, what a proud, mysterious cat.
2nd Sop.	Oh, what a proud, mysterious cat.
Alto	Oh, what a proud, mysterious cat.
Sop.	Mew, (2nd sop.) mew, (alto) mew.

Choice of a selection will be dependent in great measure upon the stage of students' literary developments. Students with strong backgrounds and interest in many facets of poetry and prose will need different types of selections than those who know little about literary works and have not developed a love for both spoken and written forms of language.

There are several stages in the development of poetic love which will affect the choice of a choral speaking selection:

I. Indifferent to Poetry

The very young child or the older child who has not been exposed to metrical language will be indifferent to it, initially. Even in high school we find students who are indifferent because of lack of exposure, unhappy experiences, or a built-up mind set against poetry.

II. Growing enjoyment of the metrical qualities of oral verse

The second stage is a growing awareness of the metrical qualities of the section of writing known as verse. For young or old the awareness is developed only through listening to poetry read aloud. To arouse this awareness in young children they should hear nursery rhymes and simple poems. Young people should be exposed to poems read either by the teacher or classmates or by means of recordings. At this stage of learning students enjoy rhythmical poems, nonsense verse, and poems with strong rhythmical patterns, usually of a humorous nature.

III. Desire to express oneself through oral and written poetry and prose

At this stage pupils love to read poetry and join in choral speaking adventures. They will respond to a widening range of literary moods. Nonsense and rhythmical verse will be much loved.

IV. **Growing enjoyment of many literary forms, especially heroic and romantic works**

As tastes develop, young people find the heroic and romantic works of the present and past of growing interest. They can identify with the characters and gain insights into the timeless and universal problems of mankind.

V. **Desire to express oneself through creative writing, creative choral speaking, interpretation, and wide reading in literary works**

Students who have had many experiences with choral speaking and have a wide range of literary interests will wish to write their own selections, develop individual interpretations of literary works, and choose their own selections. Students will need guidance in interpretations, and many sources of materials should be made available to them.

Pupil needs will vary from group to group, but these should be of prime importance when choosing choral speaking selections:

1. Choose poems that are of immediate interest to pupils. Choose those that are about things in and out of school in which children are interested vitally.
2. When choosing a series of poems, try to vary the type of poem you will use. Use some light poems, some dark poems, some comical and humorous poems, and some that are sad and solemn. Choose some poems that will interest boys, some to interest girls, some for the bright child, and some for the slow. Choose some with strong rhythmical qualities and some with little; choose some unrhymed verse and some prose.
3. Try to choose your selections from the child's point of view. What will he really like? What will appeal to him? When children can read for themselves, let them choose poems that could be used chorally.
4. If groups of pupils have particular enunciation or speech problems, poems may be selected that contain these difficulties, and skills may be developed in these areas.
5. Selections may be chosen for group work to help pupils with group and individual personal problems. They may be utilized as choral speaking bibliotherapy, whereby students will gain insights into their actions.

Where will the teacher find poetry?

During pre-service years prospective teachers should begin files of poetry and prose that will be useful for many purposes. These files should contain a collection of selections suitable for choral speaking. Many sources are available for choral speaking selections. The following list should prove useful.

Additional Readings

Reference Sources

Subject Index to Poetry for Children and Young People. Chicago: American Library Assoc., 50 East Huron Street, Chicago, Illinois.

Brewton, John E. *Subject Index to Children's Poetry.* New York: H.W. Wilson Company, 1951.

Bruncken, H. *Subject Index to Poetry.* Chicago: American Library Association, 1940.

Dixon, R. J., ed. *Granger's Index to Poetry.* New York: Columbia University Press, 1957.

Granger, Edith., ed. *Index to Poetry and Recitations.* H.H. Bessey ed., 3rd ed., Supplements to 1944. Chicago: A.C. McClurg and Company, 1940.

Hastings, Henry C. *Spoken Poetry on Records and Tapes.* Chicago: American Library Association, 1957.

Sell, Violet et al. *Subject Index to Poetry for Children and Young People.* Chicago: American Library Association, 1957.

Anthologies of Poetry for Children

Adams, F. A., and Elizabeth McCarrick. *High Days and Holidays.* New York: Dutton, 1927.

Adshead, G. L., and Annis Duff. *An Inheritance of Poetry.* Cambridge, Mass.: Houghton Mifflin and Company, 1948.

Association for Childhood Education. Literature Committee. *Sung Under the Silver Umbrella.* New York: Macmillan, 1935.

Blishen, Edward, comp. *Oxford Book of Poetry for Children.* New York: Franklin Watts Inc., 1962.

Brewton, John E. *Gaily We Parade.* New York: Macmillan, 1940.

Brewton, John E., comp. *Under the Tent of the Sky.* New York: Macmillan, 1937.

Carnegie Library School Association, comp. *Our Holidays In Poetry.* comp. by M.P. Harrington, H.W. Wilson, 1929.

De La Mare, Walter, comp., *Tom Tidder's Ground.* New York: Alfred A. Knopf, 1961.

De La Mare, Walter, comp. *Come Hither.* Alfred A. Knopf, 1960.

Edgar, M. G. ed. *A Treasury of Verse for Little Children.* New York: Thomas Y. Crowell Company.

Geismer, B. P., and A.B. Sutter. *Very Young Verses.* Boston: Houghton, 1945.

Grahame, Kenneth, ed., *The Cambridge Book of Poetry for Children.* New York: G.P. Putnams Sons, 1933.

Harrington, Mildred P. ed., *Ring-a-Round.* New York: Macmillan Company, 1960.

Hohn, Max T. ed., *Stories in Verse.* New York: Odyssey Press, 1943.

Huffard, Grace H., and Laura M. Carlisle, comp. *My Poetry Book.* Chicago: John C. Winston Company, 1934.

Ireson, Barbara, ed., *The Barnes Book of Nursery Verse*. New York: A.S. Barnes and Co., Inc., 1960.

McDonald, Gerald D. *A Way of Knowing, A collection of poems for boys*. New York: Thomas Y. Crowell Company, 1959.

Nash, Ogden. *The Moon is Shining Bright as Day*. New York: J.B. Lippincott Company, 1953.

Parker, Elinor, comp. *100 Story Poems*. New York: Thomas Y. Crowell Company, 1951.

Untermeyer, Louis, ed. *Rainbow in the Sky*. New York: Harcourt Brace and Company, 1935.

Untermeyer, Louis, ed. *Stars to Steer By*. New York: Harcourt Brace and Company, 1941.

Untermeyer, Louis, ed. *The Golden Treasury of Poetry*. New York: Golden Press, 1959.

Werner, Jane. *The Golden Book of Poetry*. New York: Simon and Schuster, 1947.

CHORAL SPEAKING SOURCES

Elementary School Selections

Bebbington, William George, and E.N. Brown, ed., *The Choir Speaks*. London: Methuen and Company, Ltd. 1952.

A choral speaking anthology.

Brown, Helen A., and Harry J. Heltman. *Let's Read Together Poems*. White Plains, New York: Row Peterson and Company, 1950.

A set of books arranged for choral reading in grades 3, 4, 5, and 6. This set should be in every school library.

Brown, Helen A., and Harry J. Heltman. *Let's Read Together Poems.* White Plains, New York: Row Peterson and Company, 1949.

    A set of books for K, 1, 2, 3. Very good set.

Dawson, Mildred A., and Mary A. Choate, *How to Help a Child Appreciate Poetry,* 828 Valencia Street, San Francisco, Calif.: Fearon Publishers, Inc., 1960.

    100 poems to express voice and action. A good book for grades two to four.

Edwards, G.N., ed. *Let's Enjoy Poetry.* Boston, Mass.: Houghton Mifflin Company, 1959.

    An anthology of children's verse for K, 1, 2, 3.

Hamm, Agnes Curren. *Choral Speaking Technique.* Milwaukee: The Tower Press, 1951.

    A similar book to Scott and Thompson's *Talking Time.*

Hemphill, Edith Irene. *Choral Speaking and Speech Improvement.* Darien, Conn., Educational Publishing Corp., 1945.

    Half of book has poems for speech improvement. A good book for someone beginning choral speaking work.

Keppie, Elizabeth Evangeline. *Speech Improvement through Choral Speaking.* Boston, Mass.: Expression Company, 1942.

    Many good poems. Poems are English and old-fashioned.

Mary, Sister Dorothy. *Choral Recitation in the Grades.* New York: Washington Dispatch, 1950.

    A book with excellent format. Poems seem a little heavy.

Rasmussen, Carrie. *Let's Say Poetry Together and Have Fun.* Minneapolis, Minn.: Burgess Publishing Company, 1962.

    For primary grades.

Rasmussen, Carrie. *Let's Say Poetry Together and Have Fun.* Minneapolis, Minn.: Burgess Publishing Company, 1963.

> For intermediate grades.

> Both books are paper backs, have colorful poems in a beautifully edited book. Books are readily useful for the teacher and children who would like to read them.

Raubicheck, Letita, *Choral Speaking is Fun.* New York: Noble and Noble Publishers, 1955.

> For primary grades.

Scott, Louise Binder, and J.J. Thompson. *Speech Ways.* St. Louis, Mo.: Webster Publishing Co., 1955.

Scott, Louis Binder, and J.J. Thompson. *Talking Time.* McGraw Hill, 2nd ed., 1966.

> A collection of poems to help child with speech difficulties. An excellent book.

Sheldon, William D. *The Reading of Poetry.* Boston: Allyn and Bacon, 1963.

> Format is good. A poetry collection.

Religious Selections

Brown, Helen Ada, and Harry J. Heltman. *Choral Reading for Worship and Inspiration.* Philadelphia: Westminster Press, 1954.

> A collection of Bible passages, great hymns, and other inspirational songs and poetry to be read or spoken aloud as a congregational part in the devotional services. This would be useful for leaders of church youth groups.

Brown, Helen A., and Harry J. Heltman. *Choral Readings from the Bible.* Philadelphia: Westminster Press, 1955.

> This would be useful with teen-agers.

Brown, Helen A., and Harry J. Heltman. *Choral Readings for Junior Worship and Inspiration.* Philadelphia: Westminster Press, 1957.

    Poems of faith for young people.

Switz, Theodore MacLean. *Great Christian Plays.* Greenwich, Conn.: Seabury Press, 1956.

    Written for choral recitation.

Junior and Senior High School Selections

Rehner, Herbert Adrian. *The Dramatic Use of Oral Interpretation and Choral Speaking.* New York: Bruce-Howard Publishing House, 1951.

    A series of choral drama numbers for youth and adults.

Robinson, Marion Parsons, and Rozetta Lura Thurston, *Poetry Arranged for the Speaking Choir.* Boston, Mass.: Expression Company, 1936.

    Useful for intellectual senior students.

Footnotes

[1] Swann, Mona, *An Approach to Choral Speech (London: Macmillan and Company, 1949), p. 45.*

[2] Rasmussen, Carrie, *Choral Speech for Speech Improvement* (Magnolia, Massachusetts: Expression Company, 1953), p. 24.

[3] *The Bible*, Matt.: 5: 2,3.

[4] Robert Browning, "Pippa's Song" from "Pippa Passes," *The Poems of Robert Browning,* (New York: Black's Reader's Service Co., 1932), p. 193.

[5] Lindsay, Vachel, "The Mysterious Cat," from the *Arbuthnot Anthology*, p. 50.

Chapter VII
YOUR ORCHESTRAL SCORE

Differing Notational Formats

Some type of notation is necessary to record suggestions or final interpretations of choral speech selections. With beginning choirs, the director, in all probability, will decide upon a certain flexible interpretation to be used during initial stages of conducting. With advanced choirs many individual and group interpretations will be discussed and practised, and finally a definite decision, especially for public performance, will be recorded. The final recording should be clearly understood and adhered to by all choir members as well as by the conductor so that a unified interpretation is possible.

This chapter presents a number of notations suitable for many types of selections. Many speakers and choir directors develop their own interpretational notations suitable for individual purposes. It is suggested that readers experiment with some of the following notations and utilize them in whole or in part according to individual needs. Simpler notations would be useful with young choirs or easy selections, whereas more difficult notations would be utilized with advanced choirs and complex selections. The interpretations of the selections are the author's, and it is possible that each reader will have different interpretations.

The accent marks as outlined in this section are based upon the ideas and beliefs of authors from the early days of choral speaking methodology. The writer believes that these notations have historical as well as practical value to some teachers today. In practice, one finds present-day teachers using some of these notations in choral speech lessons, but constant usage is open to question, and the ideas should be used sparingly to prevent mechanization of the art of choral speaking.

Simple Notations

I. Accent Marks

Scoring using only accent marks is the easiest type of notation and is basic to all types of notations. The number of feet in a line may be recorded:

Farewell to the Farm
by Robert Louis Stevenson[1]

Iambic tetrameter	Feet in lines
⏑ ´ ⏑ ´ ⏑ ´ ⏑ ´ The coach is at the door at last;	4
⏑ ´ ⏑ ´ ⏑ ´ ⏑ ´ The eager children mounting fast	4
⏑ ´ ⏑ ´ ⏑ ´ ⏑ ´ And kissing hands, in chorus sing;	4
⏑ ´ ⏑ ´ ⏑ ´ ⏑ ´ Good-bye, good-bye, to everything.	4

II. Simple Rhythm and Two Levels of Pitch

This notation presents the time signature, or underlying rhythmic structure, and two levels of pitch, high or low. The designations for levels of pitch tend to be vague, but they show that variations of a sort are intended.[2] Many writers do not approve of the arbitrary pitch, which is a false typification of normal inflectional speech.

2	1		is at the	1	2	1
The coach		2 / 1 \ 2	door	at	last

2	1	2	chil	2	1	ting	1
The	ea	ger	1	dren	moun	2	fast

2	1	2	hands	in	chor	us	1
and	kiss	ing	1	2	1	2	sing

Your Orchestral Score 67

| Good | 1 | Good | 1 | to | ev | ery | 1 | 2 rest |
| 2 | bye | 2 | bye | 2 | 1 | 2 | thing | |

III. Accent and Pitch

This notation is easy for children to understand and is a quick method of scoring. A heavy dot indicates major stress and a light dot indicates minor stress. Pitch depends upon the height of the dots above the text.[3]

The coach is at the door at last;

The eager children mounting fast

And kissing hands in chorus sing;

"Good-bye, good-bye, to everything."

IV. Varying Levels of Pitch

This is one of the easiest notations and allows for much freedom of rhythm while designating approximate levels of pitch. It may be superimposed on other notations that stress rhythmic structure. De Banke suggested four kinds of inflection in this notation:[4]

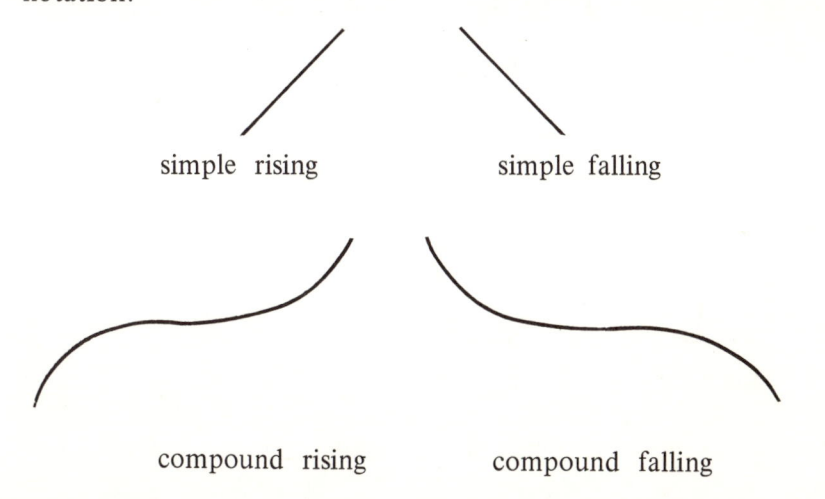

simple rising   simple falling

compound rising   compound falling

The coach is at the door at last

The eager children mounting fast

And kissing hands in chorus sing

"Good-bye, good-bye, to everything."

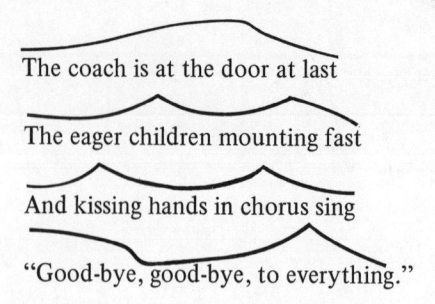

V. Ending glides

This may be used for endings of lines. The notations are:

♩ last stressed syllable a downward glide.

♩ last stressed syllable an upward glide.

In "Farewell to the Farm" the last line of the stanza might have a downward glide to suggest finality, and the third stanza an upward glide to suggest an incomplete idea.

If glides, *per se,* were taught to children, an artificiality of speaking would most likely be the result, but the teacher may discover that in certain instances a class may unconsciously use a glide to express meaning or mood and recording, and that these might be expressed by these notations.[5]

And kissing hands in chorus sing;

"Good-bye, good-bye, to everything. ♩"

Overusage of glides can produce odd results and disrupt meaning, and so this notation should be used sparingly.

Another type of glide notation has been suggested by Enfield.[6] Tone positions in pitch are designated by:

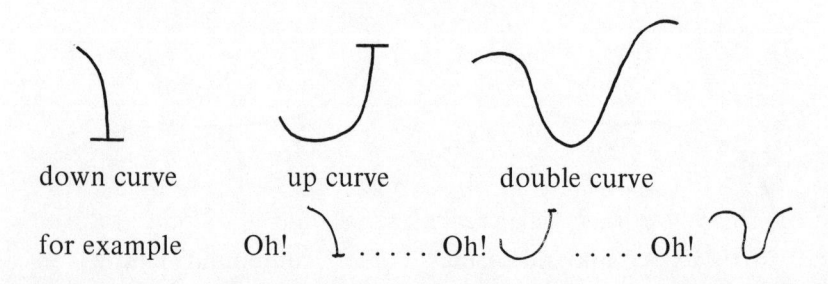

down curve   up curve   double curve

for example   Oh! ⌐......Oh! ⌣ .....Oh! ⌣⌐

VI. Varying Levels of Pitch

This notational system will be useful if you wish a beginning class to become conscious of varying levels of pitch. The basic or normal pitch is lowest, and three higher levels are designated on upper lines. Children with monotone voices may be helped if they read this type of scoring.

Levels of Pitch:

```
                                              third
                            second
                 first
basic
```

FAREWELL TO THE FARM

```
third
second
first                      is       door at
basic     The coach    at the          last.

third
second                   chil
first              ger       dren moun   ting
basic     The ea                            fast

third
second
first                ing hands in chor
basic     And kiss                  us sing

third                   good       ev
second                       bye to   ery
first     Good
basic          bye                    thing.
```

The climax of the verse in this second interpretation is expressed by the two "good-bye's" in the last line. Accents and emphases may be superimposed upon this notation, as in line two above, by means of straight lines above the syllables to be accented.[7]

Detailed Notations

Detailed notations are varied in style and should be adapted to the needs of the particular choir and director's desires.

In this section the poem "Sea Fever" has been used to illustrate the notations. Although written in first person singular, it has universal appeal and is therefore adaptable to choral groups. The rhythm of this interpretation is dactyllic octameter and is adapted from Dolman.[8]

Detailed Notation I

The following steps show how the notation was developed:

1. Determine underlying rhythmic structure and place heavy and light stress marks under syllables.
2. Determine the number of feet or major stresses in each line and write this number in right hand column.
3. Determine rests. Note that the eighth beat is a rest in each line.
4. Determine irregular stresses. Note "Wheel's kick" and "wind's song"; stress on "ing" in "flying" and "crying" has been decided as a light stress, whereas the "er" in "rover" and "over" is heavy due to placement in poem and the pronunciation stated in Webster's Dictionary.
5. Determine line rhyming patterns and mark a,b,c in right-hand column.
6. Breathing marks are designated by √
7. Volume and tempi marks are placed down the left-hand side in accordance with musical notations:

    Key:

Volume:	pp	very quiet
	p	quiet
	mp	moderately quiet
	mf	average
	f	loud
	ff	very loud
Tempo:	acc.	accelerando – getting faster
	rit.	ritardando – getting slower, gradually

8. Grouping voices into various parts is designated on left side. More detailed voicing patterns may be written over words in text.

Detailed Notation II

If there is a need to stress pitch fluctuations in choral speech, the following pattern is useful. Four pitch bands are utilized. Arrows are utilized to show further tone fluctuations, and brackets mark word clusters or thought units.[9]

	Pitch Levels	Pattern Marking
4.	High; used sometimes for special emphasis and under emotional stress	A line a space above text
3.	Range above habitual pitch	A line immediately above text
2.	Usual range; one most frequently used	A line immediately below text
1.	Range just below usual to lowest speech level	A line placed a space below text

Prose Notations

Patterns and combinations of patterns for poetry may be used with prose selections. For the individual speaker as well as for the choral group, reading of prose is facilitated by easy-to-read scores and simply-marked pages of manuscript. Ideas from the poetry section may appeal to the reader, or you may wish to utilize some of the following ideas which are useful for solo reading as well as for group recitation.

Try to design a page so that sections will stand out so that you will not lose your place in long pages of typing.

Prose Notation I

Pages of prose may be written in thought units, one unit to a line, to facilitate reading and emphasis upon meaning. More important ideas are placed toward the left of the page, and lesser ideas toward the right.

> I believe
> > in the United States of America
> as a government of the people,
> > > for the people
> > whose just powers
> > > > are derived from the consent of the governed:
>
> a democracy
> > in a republic
> > > a sovereign nation
> > > > one and inseparable
>
> established upon those principles of freedom
> > > equality
> > > > justice
> > > > > and humanity
>
> > > for which American patriots sacrificed their lives
> > > and fortunes.[10]

Prose Notation II

In this notation climax points may be marked in color or bracketed ("it is my duty to my country"). Important sentences or phrases are designated in color or underlined. Paragraphs or sections of the page are marked along the edge of the page with large dark lines. Expression notations are placed along left-hand margin.

Pages may be typed in blocks with spaces separating thought units instead of utilizing markings along the edge of the page.

▮ I believe in the United States of America, ▮

as a government of the people, for the people:

whose just powers are derived from the consent

of the governed: • a democracy in a republic: •

Your Orchestral Score

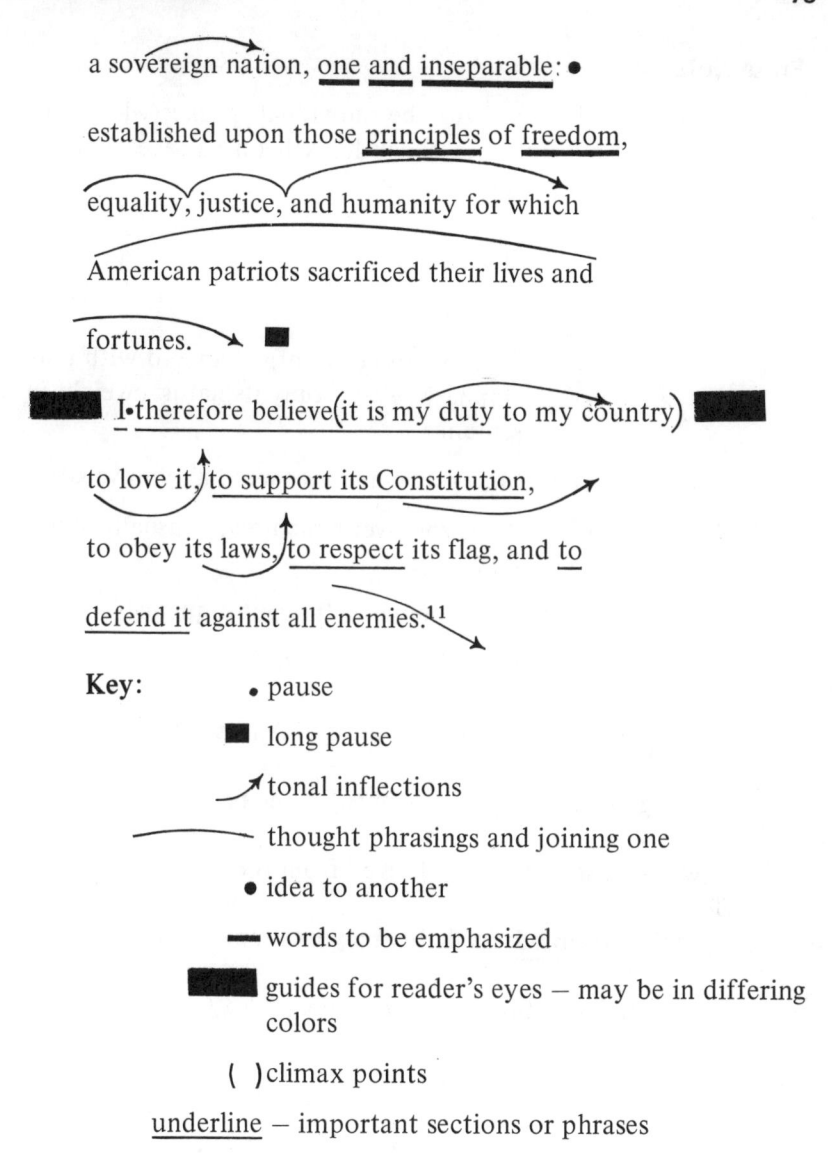

a sovereign nation, <u>one</u> and <u>inseparable</u>: •

established upon those <u>principles</u> of <u>freedom</u>,

equality, justice, and humanity for which

American patriots sacrificed their lives and

fortunes. ■

I•therefore believe (it is my duty to my country)

to love it, to support its Constitution,

to obey its laws, to <u>respect</u> its flag, and <u>to</u>

<u>defend it</u> against all enemies.[11]

Key: • pause

■ long pause

⤴ tonal inflections

——— thought phrasings and joining one
• idea to another

— words to be emphasized

■ guides for reader's eyes — may be in differing colors

( ) climax points

<u>underline</u> — important sections or phrases

This method shows pauses and inflections and presents a means of joining one thought idea to another. In the first sentence the idea of the "United States of America" standing alone loses its meaning in the context of the paragraph unless the reader consciously ties the idea in to "a government of the people" as shown by the phrase markings.

Prose Notation III

This notation is useful for the individual speaker who wishes to emphasize certain points and check himself on passages which cause enunciation and meaning difficulties.

Key:
- / Short pause
- // Longer pause
- ～～ When tempted to inflect a word with unusual emphasis, give it only its natural weight in the sentence
- = Slow down and give word all you've got
- " " A section over which reader usually stumbles. Be careful
- # Break between thought sequence
- ___ Means hit word hard[12]

I believe in the United States of America /

as a government of the people/for the people: //

whose just powers are derived from the consent

of the governed: // a democracy in a republic: //

a sovereign nation,/one and inseparable: //

established upon those principles of freedom, /

equality,/justice,/and humanity/for which

American patriots sacrificed their lives and fortunes. #

I therefore believe it is my duty to my

country//to love it,/to support its Constitution,/

to obey its laws,/"to respect its flag",/and to defend it against all enemies.

Prose Notation IV

This is a very detailed notation and causes the speaker to check correct dictionary pronunciations and pay accurate attention to stress and accent. It is of value in meticulous preparation stressing intonation and meaning. Note that the pause markings have more specific meanings than in the previous notations.

Key: / Primary stress

∩ Secondary stress

\ Tertiary stress

∪ Weak (lightest) stress

|-- Represents a break between two relatively closely related ideas

||-- Represents a break between less closely related ideas, but ideas that still belong to the same thought sequence

-- Represents a break long enough to indicate breaks between thought sequences[13]

I believe in the United States of America as a government of the people,|for the people: || whose just powers are derived from the consent of the governed:||a democracy in a republic: || a sovereign nation,|one and inseparable:||established upon those principles of freedom,|equality, justice,|and humanity for which American patriots sacrificed their lives and fortunes. #

I|therefore believe it is my duty to my country|to love it,|to support its Constitution, to obey its laws,|to respect its flag,|and to defend it against all enemies.

Farewell to the Farm
by Robert Louis Stevenson[15]

The coach is at the door at last;
The eager children, mounting fast
And kissing hands in chorus sing;
"Good-bye, good-bye, to everything."

"To house and garden, field and lawn,
The meadow gates we swung upon,
To pump and stable, tree and swing,
Good-bye, good-bye, to everything."

"And fare you well for evermore,
O ladder at the hayloft door,
O hayloft where the cobwebs cling,
Good-bye, good-bye, to everything."

Crack goes the whip, and on we go;
The trees and houses smaller grow,
Last, round the woody turn we swing:
"Good-bye, good-bye, to everything."

Sea Fever by John Masefield[16]

Volume	Tempo		Feet in line	End line rhyming pattern
All	P	I must go down to the seas again, to the lonely sea and the sky,	8	a
All	MP	And all I ask is a tall ship and a star to steer her by,	8	a
5 voices (or groups) from dark to light	MF	And the wheel's kick and the wind's song and the white sail's shaking,	8	b
	MP	And a grey mist on the sea's face and a grey dawn breaking.		
All, dark	MF Acc	I must go down to the seas again, for the call of the running tide	8	c
Dark		Is a wild call and a clear call that may not be denied;	8	c
All	F	And all I ask is a windy day with the white clouds flying,	8	b
All	Rit	And the flung spray and the blown spume and the sea-gulls crying.	8	b
All	MF Acc	I must go down to the seas again to the vagrant gypsy life,	8	d
		To the gull's way and the whale's way where the wind's like a whetted knife;	8	d
Dark	MP	And all I ask is a merry yarn from a laughing fellow-rover,	8	e
Light	P Rit	And a quiet sleep and a sweet dream when the long tick's over.	8	e

DETAILED NOTATION I

Sea Fever   by John Masefield

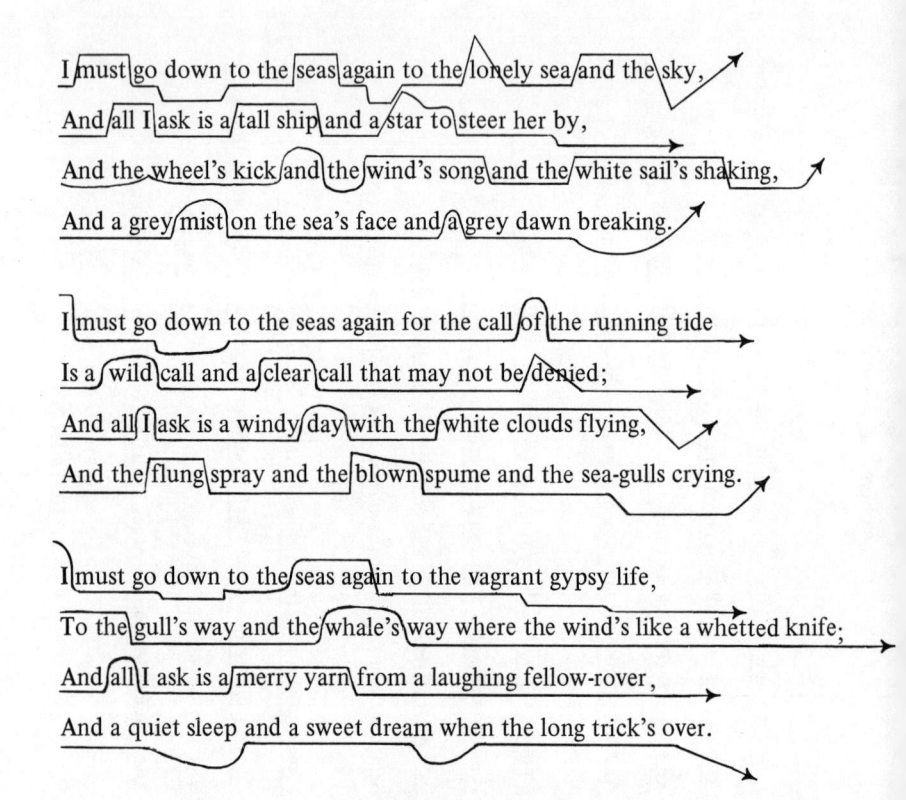

I must go down to the seas again to the lonely sea and the sky,
And all I ask is a tall ship and a star to steer her by,
And the wheel's kick and the wind's song and the white sail's shaking,
And a grey mist on the sea's face and a grey dawn breaking.

I must go down to the seas again for the call of the running tide
Is a wild call and a clear call that may not be denied;
And all I ask is a windy day with the white clouds flying,
And the flung spray and the blown spume and the sea-gulls crying.

I must go down to the seas again to the vagrant gypsy life,
To the gull's way and the whale's way where the wind's like a whetted knife;
And all I ask is a merry yarn from a laughing fellow-rover,
And a quiet sleep and a sweet dream when the long trick's over.

DETAILED NOTATION II

Footnotes

[1] Stevenson, Robert Louis, "Farewell to the Farm," from the *Arbuthnot Anthology*, p. 50.

[2] Lyon, James, *Notes on Choral Speaking* (Toronto: Clarke Irwin and Company, Ltd. 1941), p. 4.

[3] Harvel, Dorothy, and May Williams Ward, *Approach to Social Studies through Choral Speaking* (Boston: Expression Company Publishers, 1945), p. 20.

[4] De Banke, Cecile, *The Art of Choral Speaking* (Boston, Mass.: Baker's Plays, 1937), p. 79, 83.

[5] Newton, Muriel B., *The Unit Plan for Choral Reading* (Boston, Mass.: Expression Company, 1937), p. 43.

[6] Enfield, Gertrude, *Verse Choir Values and Technique* (Boston, Mass.: Expression Company, 1937), p. 43.

[7] Enfield, Gertrude, Ibid., p. 43.

[8] Dolman, John, *The Art of Reading Aloud* (New York: Harper and Brothers, 1956), p. 90.

[9] Smith, Joseph Fielding, and James R. Linn, *Skill in Reading Aloud,* (New York: Harper and Bros., 1960), p. 128.

[10] Page, William Tyler, Adopted by an Act of Congress, April 16, 1918. From *Liberty* Review and Herald Publishing Association, Washington, D.C. Vol 58:5, Sept-Oct., 1963.

[11] Ibid.

[12] Henneke, Ben Graf, *Reading Aloud Effectively,* (New York: Rinehart and Company, 1956), p. 65.

[13] Henneke, *op. cit.*

[14] Stevenson, *op. cit.*

[15] Masefield, John, "Sea Fever," from the *Arbuthnot Anthology* p. 84.

Chapter VIII

YOUR MAGIC WAND

The teacher of the verse speaking choir needs to know the fundamentals of conducting. Much can be learned by watching skilled conductors and by a systematic study of conducting techniques.

Is it possible for anyone to learn to conduct? Yes — it is possible for anyone who can read a poem with feeling to conduct a group. Anyone who has danced freely to a snatch of melody or skipped down a walk can express the bodily movement necessary for conducting.

Conducting is the bodily expression of an unspoken thought. It is a physical interpretation of rhythm and meaning which one does with the hands and in some measure with the complete body. It may be merely beating out the rhythmic structure with your magic wand. It may be guiding the inner meanings of the selection as understood by the conductor and the choir into fuller interpretation as the choir grows in skills and abilities. Conducting is listening to individuals and groups, changing tempi, rhythms, and climaxes so that the work is a varying adaptation of preconceived patterns based upon the choir's present needs. Conducting is molding the tonal patterns and moods into a unified meaningful whole.

The choral speaking conductor and the musical conductor have differing roles. The musical conductor is a leader, and the musicians interpret according to his wishes and directions. In creative choral speaking the conductor is endeavoring to help students grow in personal interpretational skills in usage of oral English. To do this, some share of interpretation must be placed in the choir's hands. Through discussions, choir members contribute interpretational ideas. At times members of the choir conduct and thus gain keener insight into actual interpretation. When choirs have gained competence or know a particular selection well, the conductor will step aside and the choir will present a selection with a student within the choir itself to be designated to start selection and guide the choir at pause and tempo changes. In creative choral speaking the conductor is a vehicle through whom the choir defines and interprets and grows in knowledge of personal interpretative skills of oral language.

The conductor needs to be able to hear patterns of speech and sound with a sensitive ear. The better the conductor's auditory discrimination of sounds, the better will be his ability to evoke subtle nuances of tonal coloring from a choir. This ability to listen to tone and speech is something which the average teacher can develop. In so doing, his personal enjoyment of the world of sound will be enhanced.

Where can one begin? Sit in your living room some evening and just listen to all the sounds around you — footfalls along a distant hall; the confident tones of a radio announcer blended with slowing rhythms of a car pulling up to a stop sign. Notice how they blend together and yet remain as separate sounds. Suddenly these sounds become background sounds to the drone of a low flying airplane and the bang of a metal storm door. The ordinary sounds are ever-changing in intensity and complexity according to the happenings around us.

As a conductor you need to be able to take the varying sounds produced by a choir and blend them into tiers of sounds, and then isolate one or another and blend them into tiers of sound again in the same way the ordinary sounds about us keep changing. Do not think of the sounds around you as one sound. Think of them as a whole, but as a whole with tiers of sounds intertwined. For instance, as you sit in your living room, there is the whole sound of all that is in your environment, but this whole is made up of many parts or tiers of sounds. The highest pitch, or tier, in the background noise may be the announcer's voice, a little lower is the metal bang of the door. You may find it difficult at first to distinguish the difference among the pitches of the car and the footfalls and the airplane. Listen carefully. Note that the car's engine has a higher whine than the drone of the airplane, and that the footfalls are much lower in pitch than any of the other sounds.

Now lean back in your arm chair again. Are you beginning to distinguish many qualities in the sounds about you? Try to pick out the clearest sounds and the dullest sounds. Listen again and note that some sounds are of longer duration than others. With practice and thought you will find that your background sounds, although unified, are in tiers of many sound colors that are constantly changing in intensity and value.

Once you become adept at listening to ordinary sounds, go to a symphony concert and listen. Listen to the qualities and tiers of tones of the various sections of the orchestra. Listen to the many blends of sounds. Note that certain types of sounds go well together; but at times odd tonal colorings are placed together, and the effect is very pleasing.

Listen to voices in group gatherings. This is where you can put some of your growing listening skills to the test. Note how voices blend or do not blend. Try to distinguish soprano, alto, tenor, and bass speaking voices. How wonderful to hear a glorious bass or a beautifully modulated soprano voice! As you begin to identify tiers of voices, try to identify tiers of sound within one voice section. This is particularly important if you will be teaching one type of voice group such as a men's chorus, boy's chorus, or an elementary school chorus. Try to distinguish the tonal levels of one of these tiers. This is fun to do on a playground where the voices all seem shrill and much the same in tonal quality, until you really listen, and then you hear groupings of tiers of tonal quality and tiers of pitch.

Of course you will be listening to plays and television and radio voices, but you need practice listening to voices in a speaking chorus. Sometimes church rituals are chanted by audiences, and this can be a fascinating listening experience if you sit quietly in a center pew and try to get the feel of emotion portrayed by the voices. Listen to good choral speaking choirs and you will gain insights into the full meaning of the beauty of speech in a choral setting.

If you are lucky enough to have a friend who plays Bach fugues, sit back and listen and listen. Can you hear all the voices as they repeat the theme and weave it into myriads of variations? If you can hear the tiers of the voices of a fugue when they are played at once in stretti, you know you have reached one of man's greatest listening zeniths — the blend of the tiers of sound as they remain individual and yet become as one.

Conducting Movements

The choral speaking conductor should portray moods and nuances of interpretation through graceful movements. Extremes should be avoided. The torso should remain relatively quiet and move in relationship to simple arm movements that are clear, precise, and readily understood by the choir.

A baton is not usually used in choral speaking, but its use is necessary if the choir is large, the selection complicated, or the presentation includes a singing choir, orchestra, or dramatic staging.

The right hand is used to depict rhythmic structure and the left to indicate changes in dynamics. The left-hand movements may rise and fall in line with the right hand or may operate independently. The left hand is an aid in developing dynamics, climaxes, tempo changes, interpretative changes, cues for attack and release, and as an indicator of breathing. At times, both hands may be used to depict rhythmic structure or dynamic changes.

The amount of arm and hand movement is usually determined by the volume required in the selection. Very loud (ff) is indicated by a movement from the eyes to the waist; moderate volume (mf) from chin to ribs; and softer dynamics (p) are indicated by wrist and hand movements alone.

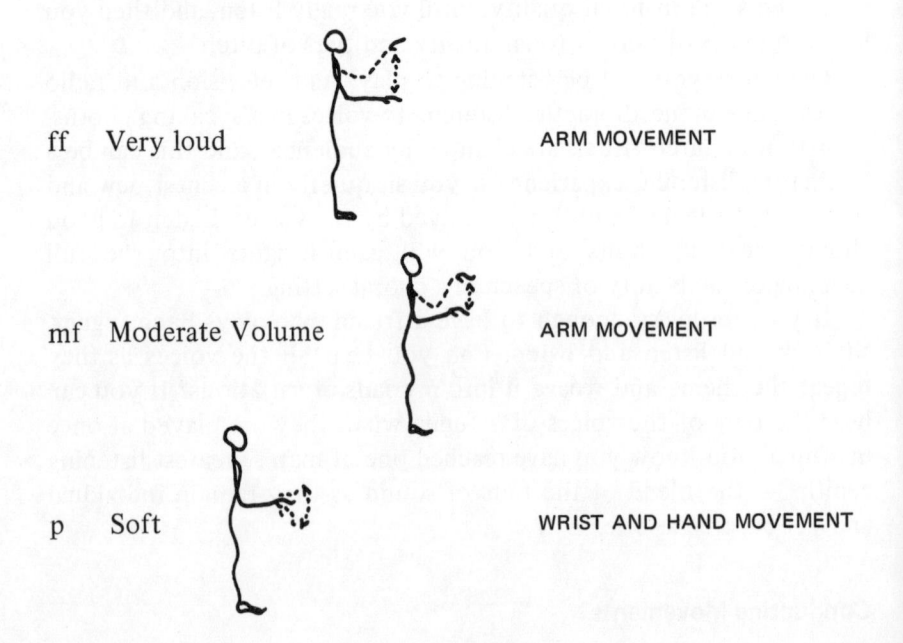

ff Very loud   ARM MOVEMENT

mf Moderate Volume   ARM MOVEMENT

p   Soft   WRIST AND HAND MOVEMENT

There are two basic conducting movements in choral speaking:
1. Sharp rhythmical movements of metrically rhymed selections which utilize *standard conducting patterns.*
2. *Free-flowing gestures* utilized in free verse, mood-inducing selections, or in metrically-rhymed selections in which rhythmical structure is minimized.

I. **Standard Conducting Patterns:**
   1. The One-Beat
   The one-beat is the simplest and consists of a straight downward movement followed by an upward movement to a rhythm or count of one.

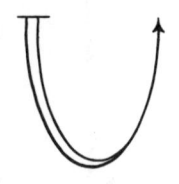

   It is used with large ideas or with a continuous simple one-type rhythm:

I'm Hiding
by Dorothy Aldis[1]

(1) I'm hiding, I'm hiding,
(2) And no one knows where
(3) For all they can see is my
(4) Toes and my hair.   rest

In the first line of 'Hiding' the first strong beat of ONE is on the first syllable of "hiding." Line 4 contains a vocal rest on the upward part of the beat. Conducting continues through the rest.

The one-beat in this selection gives a sense of flowing rhythm from line to line throughout the verse.

2. The Two-Beat
   The two-beat divides the one-beat in half with a defined break of the hand at the end of each downward and upward stroke. Movements are straight up and down and should not veer to the side. This will help distinguish the two-beat from one- or four-beat rhythms for your choir.

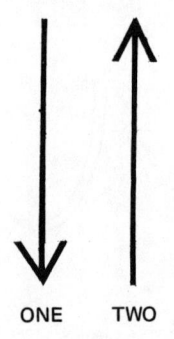

   ONE   TWO

   The two-beat is utilized in perky rhythmical selections as well as in slower, more ponderous ones. Note that the quick movements of the squirrel are depicted by the two-beat. Lines 2 and 3 contain one silent beat or rest:

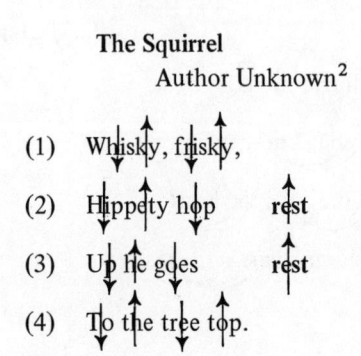

   The Squirrel
   Author Unknown[2]

   (1) Whisky, frisky,
   (2) Hippety hop   rest
   (3) Up he goes   rest
   (4) To the tree top.

3. The Three-Beat
   The three-beat consists of a downward beat which moves directly into a defined motion toward the right and completes the triangle with an upward motion.

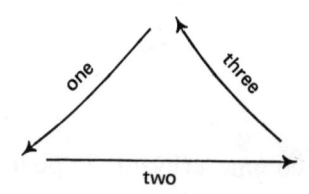

   Although the waltz rhythm of three is common in musical composition, the three-beat is rare in poetic writing. In the works of Amy Lowell and Emily Dickinson three-beat lines are interspersed with other rhythms:

	I Never Saw A Moor by Emily Dickinson[3]	Feet per line
1.	I ne/ver s/aw a Mo/or –	3
2.	I ne/ver s/aw the S/ea –	3
3.	Yet kn/ow I h/ow the He/ather looks	4
4.	And wh/at the bi/llows b/e.	3

   In the first line the three beats are on "never," "saw" and "Moor". "I" is part of the beginning upbeat. Line 3 is four beats.

4. Four-Beat
   The four-beat is characterized by a motion toward the left in the second beat, followed by a motion toward the right in the third beat.

```
                    ↖  four
     ↖        _____/___
  two  \____/_____/___↘
            ↖  one       three ↘
```

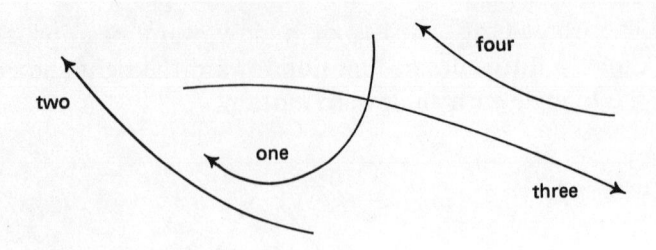

This is a common rhythm in poetic writing.

The Swing
by Robert Louis Stevenson[4]

  1   2   3   4
How do you like to go up in a swing,
 1   2   3   4
Up in the air so blue?   rest
1   2   3   4
Oh, I do think it the pleasantest thing
1   2   3   4
Ever a child can do!   rest

The fourth beat in the second and fourth line is silent.

II. Less Formalized Conducting Movements

Conducting movements may be of any number and variety and should arise from the natural feelings inherent in the selection and in the interpretation sought by the conductor and choir. The following descriptions of free conducting movements are the author's. Each conductor will need to experiment and develop those free-flowing movements that are suitable for particularized situations. Sometimes they will be combined with standard conducting movements.

The four areas which concern the conductor are inflection, volume, tempo, and phrasing. Inflection should be dealt with in discussion periods where differing meaningful ways of interpretation are explored. It should be developed individually and in

Your Magic Wand

small groups, through listening and appraising oral work. Selections may be marked as in Chapter VII, and various inflections practised. Volume, tempo, and phrasing, though begun in discussion sessions, need coordination through conducting.

Some patterns of suggested free-conducting movements follow: depending upon choir needs, the conducting movements indicated for volume could be for tonal or inflectional changes as well.

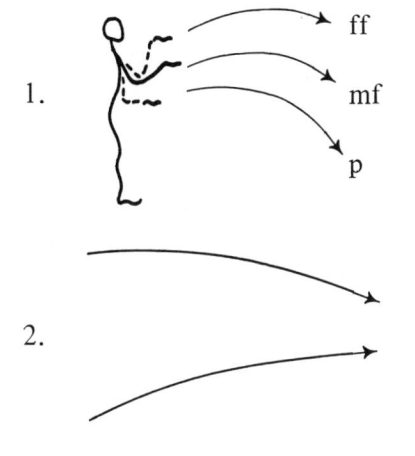

1.   ff   Movements at waistline indicate p; at chest level, mf; and at chin level, ff.
                   mf
                 p

2. Decreasing volume OR lowering of inflectional level.

    Increasing volume OR rising inflection.

3. A downward palm indicates quiet, smooth interpretation and an upward palm, stimulating interpretations.
4. Volume and grouping of words and phrases are indicated by same movement:

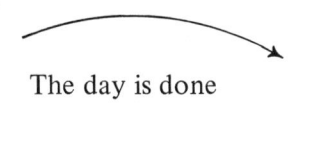

    The day is done   The left to right hand movement indicates average volume if placed at chest level, and the words would be spoken as one phrase.

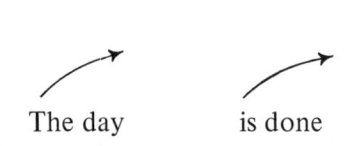

    The day   is done   In this interpretation the volume would increase, and the words would be spoken in two phrases.

5. Definite movements with palm down may indicate stressed words. To slow down a choir in which the tempo is going too fast this movement may be used.

                    ↘ ↘   ↓
                    I like   you.

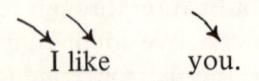

6. Fingers cupped and palms up indicate quickened tempo and stimulating interpretation.

                ↗ ↗   ↗ ↗
               Sing Hey   Sing Ho!

Four upward movements in a circular pattern might be used to indicate the desired idea:

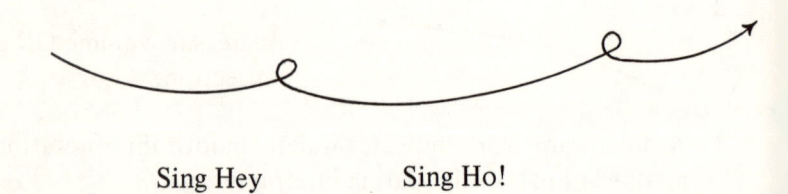

               Sing Hey   Sing Ho!

Examples of these free conducting movements utilized in prose and poetry follow:

In "Evening Hymn" volume and smooth grouping of words is indicated. Backward and forward sweeps of the hand are used with a downward palm.

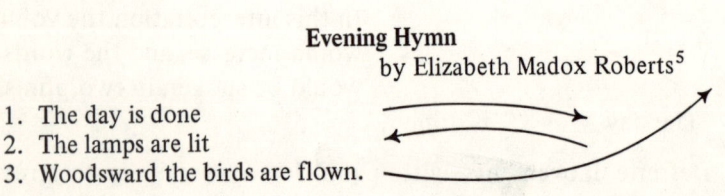

Evening Hymn
by Elizabeth Madox Roberts[5]

1. The day is done
2. The lamps are lit
3. Woodsward the birds are flown.

In line one a decreasing volume is indicated from "day is done." In line 2 the volume will remain even, and in line 3 the volume will rise. The smooth sweep of the conducting pattern indicates that all lines will be spoken in one breath as single thought units.

Volume or inflection remains steady throughout. Phrasing of prose lines is indicated. Conducting movements would not be all to the right; alternate gestures would be to the left. In the diagrams R indicates a right-to-left movement and L a left-to-right movement. Whether these would be left-to-right or right-to-left or oblique or horizontal or vertical would depend upon final style developed by conductor and understood by the choir.

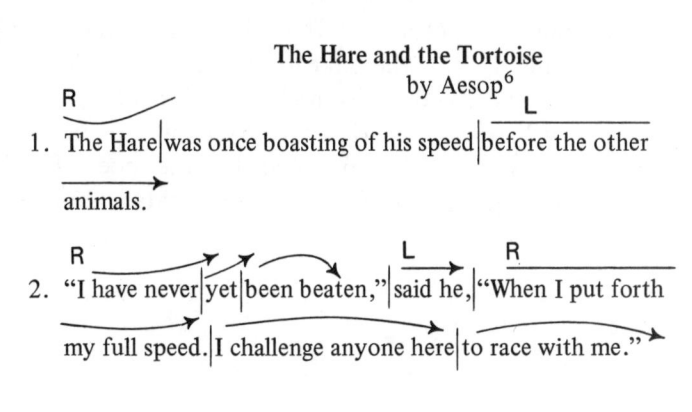

The Hare and the Tortoise
by Aesop[6]

1. The Hare | was once boasting of his speed | before the other animals.

2. "I have never | yet | been beaten," | said he, | "When I put forth my full speed. | I challenge anyone here | to race with me."

Prelude I
by T. S. Eliot[7]

1. The winter evening settles down

2. With smell of steaks in passageways

3. Six o'clock.

The first two lines have broad sweep of the hand, but three steady downward hand movements would be used in line 2. The "o' " would be a faster movement than "six" and "clock."

Smooth phrasing in prose selections is a necessity. An interpretation for Ps. 147[8] might be:

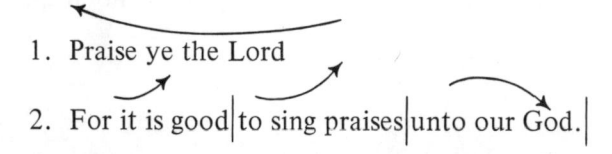

1. Praise ye the Lord

2. For it is good | to sing praises | unto our God. |

In line one the mood is happy and tonal level rises. Line two has two bright upward-moving phrases, followed by a final, more solemn phrase with descending tonal level.

Stresses and Accents

In musical writing it is usual to give certain beats more stress than others. In two-beat time the first beat is traditionally stressed. In four-beat time the first beat receives heaviest stress with the second, third, and fourth beats receiving, in order, descending amounts of stress.

The choral speaking conductor will find that any attempt to follow such stresses, merely for the sake of the basic rhythmical structure of the poem, will cause dire rhythmical results and also lose the poetic meaning. Utilize the underlying rhythm of a poem as a backdrop to the inherent meaning intended by the poet. Read "Silver" with exaggerated accents on first and third beats and notice how the meaning is distorted.

Silver
by Walter de la Mare[9]
ONE   2   three   4
Slowly, silently, now the moon
ONE   2   three   4
Walks the night in her silver shoon:
ONE   2   three   4
This way, and that, she peers, and sees
ONE   2   three   4
Silver fruit upon silver trees!

Listen to poorly-trained amateur musicians sit on each so-called accented beat and then listen to accomplished musicians play the same selection. You will discover that professionals cause you to be aware of the rhythmical structure, but the mood meaning of the music receives prime emphasis. This must be the goal in choral speaking as well.

In certain poems, especially doggerel and fun-type poems, standard accenting adds to the meaning and understanding of the poem. In "The Squirrel" a quick accent on the first beat gives the whimsical note necessary for this interpretation, as does the accenting of the one and three beats in "Higgledy Piggledy".

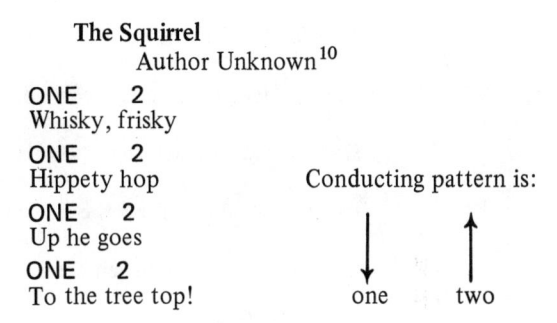

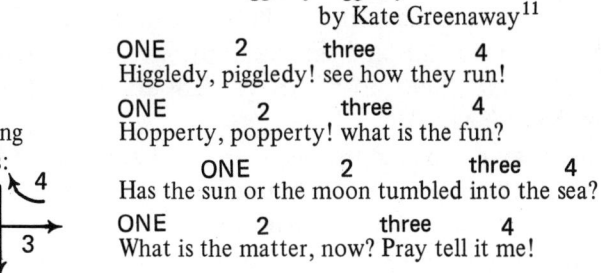

The Squirrel
Author Unknown[10]

ONE 2
Whisky, frisky
ONE 2
Hippety hop
ONE 2
Up he goes
ONE 2
To the tree top!

Conducting pattern is:

↓ ↑
one two

Higgledy Piggledy
by Kate Greenaway[11]

ONE 2 three 4
Higgledy, piggledy! see how they run!
ONE 2 three 4
Hopperty, popperty! what is the fun?
ONE 2 three 4
Has the sun or the moon tumbled into the sea?
ONE 2 three 4
What is the matter, now? Pray tell it me!

Conducting pattern is:

In "The Sandpiper" rhythmical conducting distorts mood and meaning. An underlying rhythmic pattern is necessary to depict the movement of picking up the driftwood and the flitting of the bird, but it should be read in prose style with slight feeling for the rhythmic structure.

The Sandpiper
by Celia Thaxter[12]

Feet in line — 4

Across the narrow beach we flit,

One little sandpiper and I,   **rest**

And fast I gather bit by bit,

The scattered driftwood bleached and dry,

The wild waves reach their hands for it,

The wild wind raves and the tide runs high,

As up and down the beach we flit, —

One little sandpiper and I.   **rest**

The Attack and Release

A teacher should utilize the conducting movements that best suit individual needs. For the teacher who has difficulty getting a choir to attack and release together, the following ideas are presented. However, once the mechanics of this method have been learned, the teacher should adapt them to particular situations and develop variants of the basic idea.

The choral speaking choir must begin and end selections precisely together. The attack should be clearly understood by all. Hesitations and indecisiveness should be avoided. In order for the choir to develop confidence and move into the selection with ease, the same initial conducting movements should be used.

In the few moments before the attack the conductor may set the mood for the selection by talking to the choir about the theme, by facial gesture, or by means of suggestions such as to "begin quickly and brightly" or "show the sadness in your eyes."

The choir's first words should be spoken on a column of exhaled air. A second before the attack or preliminary upbeat, the conductor should smile at the choir and take a breath while beginning the first conducting movement. The choir will automatically breathe with him and say the first words with full breath support.

Preliminary Upbeat

The upbeat is a preliminary movement to get the choir ready to speak on the first downbeat of conducting. It is the "Get Set", "Get Ready" movement before the "Go" of the first downbeat.

The Upbeat — when selection begins on the first metrical foot of line.

The placement of the preliminary upbeat corresponds to the conducting patterns for the various rhythms.

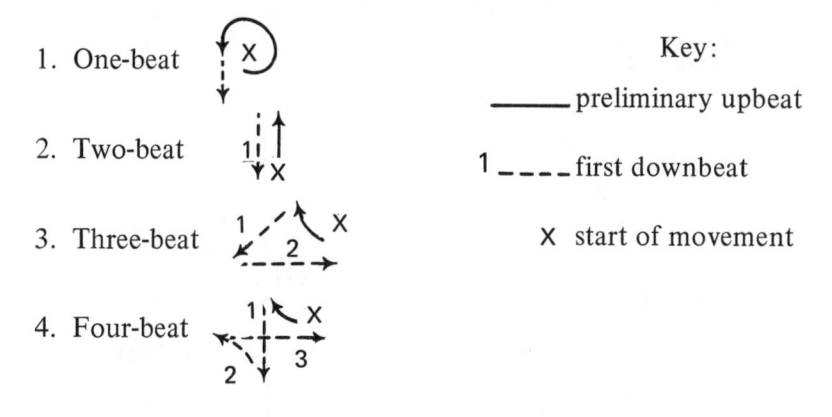

1. One-beat

2. Two-beat

3. Three-beat

4. Four-beat

Key:

――――― preliminary upbeat

1 _ _ _ _ first downbeat

X start of movement

5. In non-metrical selections or in selections where the metrical structure will be minimized, a simple preliminary upbeat similar to that of the four-beat is followed by a clearly defined downbeat.

Both hands may move together on the preliminary upbeat and first downbeat, or the right hand may present the upbeat and the left join at the beginning of the first downbeat. The latter method is helpful to cue in a choir and stress the importance of the first downbeat.

The preliminary upbeat sets the tempo of the selection. A slow, ponderous selection will have a slow, ponderous preliminary upbeat, and a fast selection will have a fast preliminary upbeat.

The preliminary upbeat also sets beginning volume. A wide sweeping gesture will indicate greater initial volume than a small gesture.

The Upbeat — when selection does not begin on first metrical foot of line.

The preliminary upbeat comes ONE BEAT AHEAD of the FIRST WORD in the selection, and the conductor begins his conducting on the beat ahead of the first word.

In "My Shadow" the first word "I" begins at the end of the fourth beat of the rhythmical structure. The preliminary beat occurs on the third beat to enable the choir to breathe on the third beat and attack the "I" on the fourth beat. The left hand may be utilized on the fourth beat to help the choir come in together on the "I."

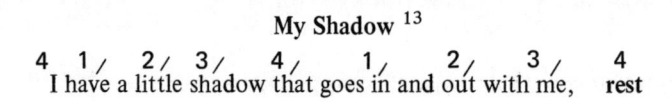

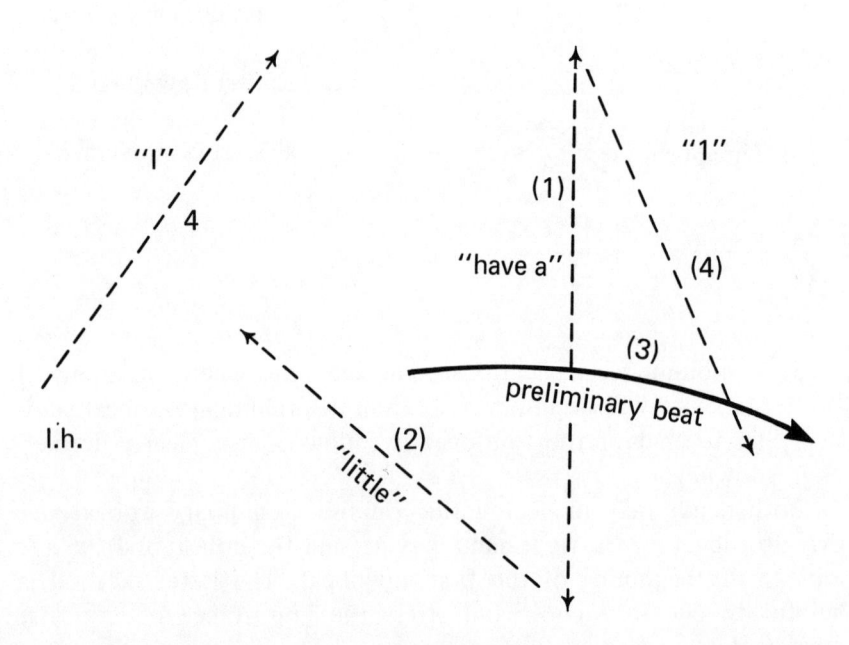

My Shadow [13]

4 1/ 2/ 3/ 4/ 1/ 2/ 3/ 4
 I have a little shadow that goes in and out with me, rest

Sometimes the traditional conducting pattern of music is not as effective in choral speaking as a variant. In "Farewell to the Farm" by R.L. Stevenson the preliminary beat may be given by a slow, slightly curving movement of the right hand, joined by the left when the first word is spoken. The author has found this variant useful if a slight pause occurs between the preliminary beat and the first word.

Your Magic Wand

Farewell To The Farm
by Robert Louis Stevenson

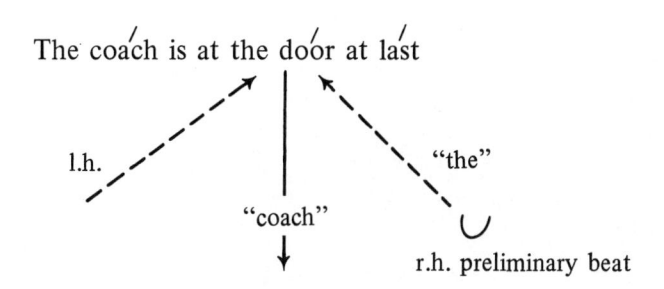

The coách is at the doór at laśt

l.h.
"coach"
"the"
r.h. preliminary beat

All attacks and releases should be practised many times until the choir responds with ease, and each director will find that certain methods are better for him than others. Some conductors prefer following the strict metrical conducting of music, and others prefer to develop their own variations. The author believes that variants are best for choral speaking classes.

The Release

The release in choral speaking is relatively easy because no time duration is necessary as in music. A simple release is to move the hand horizontally away from the body gradually touching finger tips to thumb tip. When finger tips meet, choir enunciates last sound of final word. The right hand or both hands together may be used.

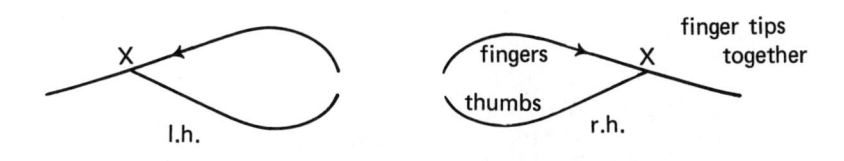

l.h.

fingers
thumbs
r.h.

finger tips together

Some conductors prefer a release ending in a downward movement and a quick circular cut-off executed with both hands on final word.

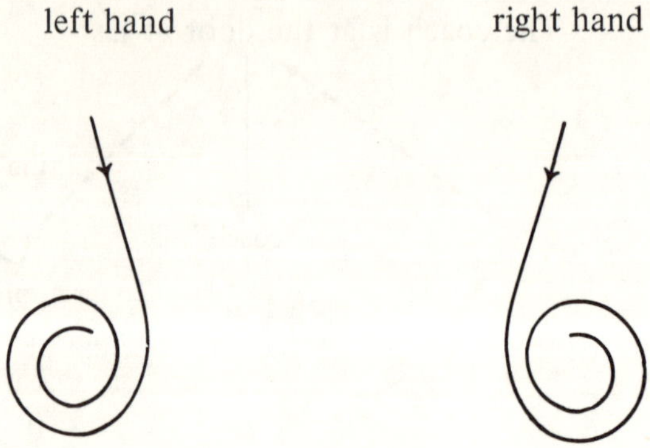

left hand   right hand

I Never Saw a Moor
by Emily Dickinson[14]

I never saw a Moor —
I never saw the Sea —
Yet know I how the Heather looks
And what the billows be.

I never spoke with God
Nor visited in Heaven —
Yet certain am I of the spot
As if the chart were given.

The Heart asks Pleasure — first —
And then — Excuse from Pain —
And then — those little Anodynes
That deaden suffering.

And then — to go to sleep —
And then — if it should be
The will of its Inquisitor
The liberty to die.

Footnotes

[1] Aldis, Dorothy, "I'm Hiding," from the *Arbuthnot Anthology* p. 107.

[2] Author Unknown, "The Squirrel," from the *Arbuthnot Anthology*, p. 56.

[3] Dickinson, Emily, "I Never Saw a Moor," from *Poems of Emily Dickonson,* ed. Thomas H. Johnson (Bleknap Press of Harvard University Press, 1955), p. 742.

[4] Stevenson, Robert Louis, "The Swing," *A Child's Garden of Verses* (New York: Charles Scribner and Sons, 1955), p. 40.

[5] Roberts, Elizabeth Madox, "Evening Hymn," from the *Arbuthnot Anthology,* p. 396.

[6] Aesop, *Fables,* "The Hare and the Tortoise," from the *Arbuthnot Anthology,* p. 230.

[7] Prelude I, T.S. Eliot.

[8] *The Bible,* Psalm 147.

[9] De La Mare, Walter, "Silver," *Collected Poems,* 1901, 1918 (New York: Henry Holt and Company, Inc.), p. 49.

[10] Author Unknown, "The Squirrel," *op. cit.*

[11] Greenaway, Kate, "Higgledy-Piggledy," *Under the Window* (London: Frederick Warne and Company, 1910), p. 37.

[12] Lowell, Amy, "Patterns," *A Shard of Silence,* ed. G.R. Ruihley, (New York: Twayne Publishers, Inc., 1957), p. 413.

[13] Stevenson, Robert L., "My Shadow," *A Child's Garden of Verses* (New York: Charles Scribner and Sons, 1955), p. 55.

[14] Dickinson, Emily, *op. cit.*

Chapter IX

TALKING TOGETHER IN THE CLASSROOM

Class Organization

As part of the oral communication section of the language arts program, choral speaking should be included in classroom activities and integrated into the total curriculum. Some teachers prefer to plan for choral speaking at a certain period in the day and follow with short reviews and drills until the selections are mastered. The writer believes this plan is useful, at times, in upper grades with pupils who have long concentration spans, but in most instances oral communication skills are better developed in short periods spaced frequently throughout the school day. A time blocking of choral speaking tends to set it apart as a special subject, non-integrated into the total curriculum.

Both choral speaking and choral singing should be spontaneous expressions of emotions as realized by pupils throughout the day. Ideally, pupils should burst into song or poetic verse as the need to do so arises.

Singing and choral speech, when integrated into the classroom, have the power to change moods and attitudes, change dull days into bright days, change distrubed children into happy children, and to improve oral communication skills.

How is this done? Let us suppose that Miss McGee, a grade three teacher, has planned to teach "Indian Children"[1] to her class. From 9:00 to 9:15 each morning her class discusses events of interest in the world around them, and recently they have been talking about where Indians live today. To introduce the poem Miss McGee utilizes five minutes of the discussion period. She shows a map of Indian tribes of long ago, and pupils compare this with a present-day map of Indian reserves. Then Miss McGee reads the poem to the class.

At 10:15 in the morning she switches from one arithmetic group to another. The children move from one place in the room to another while reciting a poem or singing a song. After the change to new groups is made and before the next group lesson begins, she asks if any child remembers anything about the poem she read earlier. She repeats the complete poem, and as she says the first stanza again, the children try to say it with her. All this has taken two or three minutes, and the children are now ready for the new class and have learned some of the poem.

As the children are putting on boots and overshoes for the noon departure, she may repeat the poem, and the children will say as much as they can remember with her. Can't you see them trudging home at noon repeating, "Where we walk to school each day, Indian children used to play?"

In the afternoon after the physical education class all may be resting quietly, and Miss McGee uses this time to teach the last two verses. In this manner the poem is learned with little effort and becomes part of the living experiences of the school day. Happy are the children who live in a classroom where poetry and song are natural concomitants of all learning activities.

Choral speech may be utilized in many ways in the classroom:

I. **To facilitate breaks between classes**

When children are changing from group to group, moving from one activity to another, a song or chorally spoken verse will help make the transition smoother. The "Grand Old Duke of York" and "Ferry Boats" are suitable.

The Grand Old Duke of York
Author Unknown[2]

The grand Old Duke of York
    He had ten thousand men,
He marched them up a very high hill
    And he marched them down again.
And when he was up he was up
    And when he was down he was down
And when he was only half way up
    He was neither up nor down.

Ferry Boats
by James S. Tippett[3]

Over the river,
Over the bay,
Ferry-boats travel
Every day.

Most of the people
Crowd to the side
Just to enjoy
Their ferry-boat ride.

Watching the seagulls,
Laughing with friends,
I'm always sorry
When the ride ends.

II. To keep children interested on long field trips on buses or walking tours

Walking tours and bus trips have times when song or choral speaking will keep the group happy and give the group unity. In classes where verse speaking has been an integral part of daily living, pupils will burst into verse, spontaneously, as they travel along. At these times a teacher may feel a warm glow of reward as snatches of rhyme come to her ears from various groups of children. The author remembers two little boys on a bus trip quietly watching the landscape roll by and repeating Robert Louis Stevenson's "Travel" while two solemn-eyed girls leaned over the adjoining seat in silent wonderment.

Travel
by Robert Louis Stevenson[4]

I should like to rise and go
Where the golden apples grow; —
Where below another sky
Parrot islands anchored lie,
And, watched by cockatoos and goats,
Lonely Crusoes building boats; —
Where in sunshine reaching out
Eastern cities, miles about,
Are with mosque and minaret
Among sandy gardens set,
And the rich goods from near and far
Hang for sale in the bazaar; —

III. To quiet high strung nerves

In our modern city living many children come into the classroom unable to function well until the cares and worries of the outside-the-classroom-world have been put aside. A beautiful poem read or repeated softly will help children to relax and settle into the day's activities. At times in the classroom tensions will arise, and again poetry, as well as song, will smooth over the rough places. "The Song my Paddle Sings" by Pauline Johnson is good for young children, and intermediate grade children love "The Day Will Bring Some Lovely Thing" by Grace Noll Crowell:

excerpts from The Song my Paddle Sings
by Pauline Johnson[5]

West wind, blow from your prairie nest,
Blow from the mountains, blow from the west.
The sail is idle, the sailor too;
O' wind of the west, we wait for you.
Blow, blow!
I have wooed you so,
But never a favour you bestow.
You rock your cradle the hills between,
But scorn to notice my white lateen.

I stow the sail, unship the mast:
I wooed you long but my wooing's past;
My paddle will lull you into rest.
O! drowsy wind of the drowsy west,
Sleep, sleep,
By your maintain steep,
Or down where the prairie grasses sweep!
Now fold in slumber your laggard wings,
For soft is the song my paddle sings.

The Day Will Bring Some Lovely Thing
by Grace Noll Crowell[6]

"The day will bring some lovely thing,"
I say it over each new dawn:
"Some gay, adventurous thing to hold
Against my heart when it is gone."
And so I rise and go to meet
The day with wings upon my feet.

I come upon it unaware —
Some sudden beauty without name:
A snatch of song — a breath of pine —
A poem lit with golden flame:
High-tangled bird notes — keenly thinned —
Like flying color in the wind.

No day has ever failed me quite —
Before the grayest day is done,
I come upon some misty bloom
Or a late night of crimson sun.
Each night I pause — remembering
Some gay, adventurous, lovely thing.

IV. To begin and end activities.

Very young children enjoy a finger play to begin story time or lessons:

Here Are Grandmother's Glasses
Author Unknown[7]

Here are grandmother's glasses
(Circle thumb and finger, each hand, over eyes)
Here is grandmother's hat.
(Fingertips together on head)
This is the way she folds her hands and puts them in her lap.

This cheery antiphonal selection is good for the end of a day:

School is Over
by Kate Greenaway[8]

School is over
Oh, what fun!
Lessons finished,
Play begun.
Who'll run fastest,   In couplets antiphonally
You or I?
Who'll laugh loudest?
Let us try.

How many poems should a class be taught? The living on-going type of choral speaking suggested in this chapter causes children and teachers to develop a wealth of loved and memorized poems. Children are free to suggest poems and to use them in daily classroom experiences. The teacher is continually bringing new poems to class attention. The number of poems learned is not important. What is important is how many of these become part of the child's living experience. Some poems are discarded, some are repeated daily for months, and some become loved and remembered throughout a life time.

Memorization

Choral speaking is a painless means of memorization. Selections are committed to memory by most pupils without any awareness of the act of memorization.

The teacher should make a conscious attempt to facilitate memorization and should not leave memorization to chance. Some selections, because of meaning and rhythmic qualities, will be memorized readily, others will be more difficult. Specific plans should be laid to help pupils learn difficult sections.

Some selections will not be deemed by the teacher and class as worthy of memorization because they are of transient value. Poems that lack appeal after a few attempts should not be memorized; but if the teacher believes they have intrinsic value for the children, she may reintroduce them at a later date when pupils are ready to accept the material.

The poems that are memorized are usually considered of lasting value by the pupils, and only by exposing pupils to many poems and using trial and error can one discover which should be retained and which discarded. Perhaps the best rule of thumb is to memorize the best-loved poems. Happily, through choral speaking, these usually "memorize themselves."

Choral speaking lessons that are short, spread throughout the day, and integrated into the classroom living patterns are usually more readily learned than selections learned in long class periods. Spaced repetition of learning is the effective factor.

The most effective time plan for memorization is: Learning........

............Quick Recall..

.....Longer Spaced Repetition..
....Much Longer Spaced

Repetition

If the learning has not been effective and is not retained, the spacing between repetitions should be shortened.
A plan for six days to learn poem S might be:

Day 1
9:10 a.m.   10:15 a.m.   Noon   3:00 p.m.
S........................S....................S..................S.....

Day 2
S ....S...................S......

Day 3
..................S... S...............

Day 4
....S...............

Day 5
.... no repetition.............................

Day 6
.... S.....

Each selection should be approached as a meaningful whole. Read or let the children read the poem, initially, as a whole. While learning sections, constantly go back and reread complete selection and complete verses. If children learn a poem line by line and verse by verse, they tend to know, not a poem, but a series of unrelated lines, or unrelated verses.

To help children learn a few difficult lines reemphasize the wholeness of these lines within the complete poem as follows:

1. Whole
2. Verse
3. Separate lines
4. Whole
5. Separate lines
6. Separate lines
7. Verse
8. Separate lines
9. Separate lines
10. Whole

Oral Reading Skills

Choral speaking is one way to help children become competent in reading. Many of the abilities necessary for good choral speaking are the skills needed for good oral reading. Dolman stated:

> Reading aloud, ..., has an important and honorable place in modern life. Educationally, it is essential as a part of the total process of learning to read well, whether to oneself or to others. Culturally, it is one of the most powerful instruments we have for the nurture of good individual minds and for collective enjoyment and appreciation of the finest products of those minds.[9]

In this endeavor toward excellence in oral reading, choral speaking plays a significant part. Through choral speaking classes pupils learn, in group situations, all the skills necessary for good oral reading. These include:

1. Meaningful interpretation of written materials.
2. Ability to transfer individual interpretation to an audience.
3. Ability to react to audience mood and vary original interpretation to meet particular situations.
4. Personal enjoyment in reading to others.
5. An easy-poised attitude.
6. Ability to read and look up at audience from time to time.
7. Variety and appropriateness of tone and speed.
8. Pleasant intonation.
9. Clear intonation.

Good oral reading has two necessary preconsiderations:
1. It must be prepared before presentation.
2. It must be read to someone in an audience situation.

The choral speaking class meets both these requirements. Pupils select, discuss, and try many patterns and arrangements of a new poem. The finalized version is the result of much thought, experimentation, and discussion.

In choral speaking the teacher should teach for transfer of oral skills to individual reading situations. Discussons centered about, "How should WE interpret this passage?" should include questions such as, "How would YOU interpret this passage if you were reading alone?".

Halting, meaningless readings of reports, news items, and basal reading materials have no place in a modern-day classroom. Oral reading of children's readers is no longer the old-fashioned "round-robin" type in which each child takes his turn reading a line or a page. Today, children choose favorite passages, practise them orally with one or more critical listeners, and then present selections to the class. Often they choose a prose section from a reader as a selection to be learned for the choral speaking class. They plan ways in which the selection may be interpreted and work in groups developing interpretations for various passages. The teacher will bring all the class together for whole class practices, or she will work with individuals who need special coaching. Solo and line-a-child sections of choral speaking give opportunities for individual help in a natural setting where all can readily understand the reason for good oral interpretation. Antiphonal settings of selections may utilize one voice opposite a choir of voices, or two voices may enter into a dialogue. Pupils should be encouraged to obtain oral reading practice at home and in community activities. Slow readers in upper grades will enjoy practising oral reading from simple children's story books if they are allowed to read these stories to kindergarten and grade one classes. They may also enjoy presenting choral speaking selections in which there are opportunities for individual interpretations.

In actual life situations much oral reading must be done after a quick perusal of the material. After pupils have become adept in creative interpretations of poems, short selections may be given to groups and individuals for short perusal and quck presentations. These presentations should be followed by discussions about better ways to prepare quickly for oral reading, ways of finding main ideas, and pitfalls of interpretation to avoid.

As oral reading skills develop in individual and group situations, reader's theater groups, especially in upper grades, may be the natural outcome. Choral speaking thus lends itself to individual as well as group oral communication skills.

Creativity in Choral Speaking

The ultimate goal in teaching choral speaking is creative interpretation by pupils. With young children, children with monotone voices, young people from backgrounds of sparse English speech, it is wise to read poems to the children and have them copy; but as soon as possible the inflectional and interpretational patterns should be worked out by the choir itself.

The conductor should pre-plan his own interpretation, but his role should be that of a guide and resource person who helps children express orally the inner feelings of the poetry they love. The conductor should respect all pupils' abilities to feel and interpret selections.

A choir needs to develop a feeling of unity in pitch, tone, mood, and purpose. The members need to develop the habit of thinking together and doing things together. Groups of the choir should work together under a group leader, on differing sections, and develop group ideas of interpretation. Much discussion is needed to assure agreement about climaxes, denouements, feeling, and mood. "What is essential above everything is that the member of a speaking choir should be free to contribute his or her own best judgment or artistic capacity to the whole effort, whether of preliminary discussion or actual interpretation."[10]

Indian Children
by Annette Wynne [11]

Where we walk to school each day
Indian children used to play
All about our native land
Where the shops and houses stand.

And the trees were very tall,
And there were no streets at all,
Not a church and not a steeple,
Only the woods and Indian people.

Only wigwams on the ground,
And at night bears prowling around —
What a different place today
Where we live and work and play.

Travel
by Robert Louis Stevenson
From A Child's Garden of Verses

I should like to rise and go
Where the golden applies grow; —
Where below another sky
Parrot islands anchored lie,
And watched by cockatoos and goats,
Lonely Crusoes building boats; —
Where in sunshine reaching out
Eastern cities, miles about,
Are with mosque and minaret
Among sandy gardens set,
And the rich goods from near and far
Hang for sale in the bazaar: -
Where the Great Wall round China goes,
And on one side the desert blows,
And with bell and voice and drum,
Cities on the other hum; —
Where are forests, hot as fire,
Wide as England, tall as a spire,
Full of apes and cocoa-nuts
And the negor hunters' huts; —
Where the knotty crocodile
Lies and blinks in the Nile,
And the red flamingo flies
Hunting fish before his eyes; —
Where in jungles, near and far,
Man-devouring tigers are,
Lying close and giving ear
Lest the hunt be drawing near,
Or a comer-by be seen
Swinging in a palanquin; —
Where among the desert sands

Some deserted city stands,
All its children, sweep and prince,
Grown to manhood ages since,
Not a foot in street or house,
Not a stir of child or mouse,
And when kindly falls the night,
In all the town no spark of light.
There I'll come when I'm a man
With a camel caravan;
Light a fire in the gloom
Of some dusty dining-room;
See the pictures on the walls
Heroes, vights, and festivals;
And in a corner find the toys
Of the old Egyptian boys.

Footnotes

[1] Wynne, Annette, "Indian Children," from *For Days and Days* (Philadelphia: J.B. Lippincott Co., 1919, 1957).

[2] Unknown Author, "The Grand Old Duke of York." from the Arbuthnot *Anthology,* p. 94.

[3] Tippett, James S., "Ferry Boats," from the Arbuthnot *Anthology,* p. 83.

[4] Stevenson, Robert Louis, "Travel," from *A Child's Garden of Verses* p. 47.

[5] Johnson, Pauline, "The Song My Paddle Sings," from *Flint and Feather* (Toronto: Musson Book Company, Ltd., 1931), p. 31.

[6] Mitchell, Lucy Sprague, "The Day Will Bring Some Lovely Thing," *Another Here and Now* (New York: E.P. Dutton and Co., Inc., 1937), p. 208.

[7] Unknown Author, "Here are Grandmother's Glasses," fingerplay.

[8] Greenaway, Kate, "School is Over," from *Under the Window,* (New York: Frederick Warne and Co., 1910), p. 92.

[9] Dolman, John, *The Art of Reading Aloud* (New York: Harper and Brothers, 1956), p. 19.

[10] Gullan, Marjorie, *The Speech Choir* (New York: Harper and Brothers, 1937), p. 23.

[11] Wynne, *op. cit.*

Chapter X
VOICE PRODUCTION

A knowledge of the basic principles of voice production is necessary for the choral speaking conductor and the choral speaking choir. The quality of choral speaking is dependent upon sensible application of these principles. The basic principles should be understood by all, but not all children should be taken through a series of voice-training lessons. Many children will speak correctly, and an occasional lesson on some particular articulatory or breathing problem will suffice.

To determine whether children need little speech training, help in specific areas, or help from specialized sources, learn to listen carefully to speech patterns. Try to establish in your own listening mind what is normal for children at varying age levels. Young children will have deviations with sounds that are difficult for their age level to pronounce. Boys' groups will tend to be slower in development than groups of girls.

Attune your ear to regional differences you may have acquired. If these are noticeable deviations from the standard American pattern, bring the sounds to your own level of consciousness so that you can hear them in your own speaking voice and in the voices of others. Develop articulatory and breathing methods to overcome the difficulty. Some speech deviations may be common to your particular school and neighborhood, and you may wish to study ways to help children with these problems.

The child with serious speech defects such as stuttering or abnormal baby-talk should be referred to a speech clinic. The classroom teacher should not attempt to deal with these because more harm than good can be done by amateur voice specialists.

Consider a child in need of special help if his speech deviation is noticeable to the listener, and if the difficulty handicaps the child in normal oral communication with others. The child who is understood only by parents and playmates at four or five years of age is in need of specialized help.

During choral speaking certain speech abnormalities, especially stuttering, will tend to disappear, and the choral speaking class will be an excellent part of the child's therapy treatments. Berry stated, "Group speaking, in which there is usually no responsibility for the proposition and shared responsibility for the evocation, is almost always associated with fluent speaking."[1]

The teacher must develop a mental ideal, a mental sound picture of good speech. The sharper the mental picture, the better one's abilities to help students acquire good speaking voices. All fine orchestral conductors have this inner ideal sound, so have choral speaking and choral singing leaders. It is something that can be developed through listening carefully, over the years, to voices and blends of voices. It is a goal toward which all strive. It is the elusive perfection without which artistic creations in sound cannot be conceived or developed. Without it your teaching will be mundane, with it your teaching will rise to unknown heights, especially if you can enable your students to catch a glimpse, even a fleeting glimpse, of what the mental ideal really is.

Breathing Techniques

"Always speak on the air cushion" is a maxim for beautiful speech. Good tonal quality rests upon a solid cushion of exhaled air. A great amount of air is not needed; but a steady amount of air constantly under, or cushioning the words, causes the tone to float on the air. Children need to discover the difference in tonal quality between speaking on the air and speaking with little air. Let as much air out of the lungs as possible and recite a line of a poem. Listen to the thin nonresonant tone. Then speak on a full column of air. Help children to listen to the difference. Once pupils become aware of the mechanics of breathing and try to breathe correctly, class tone will gradually improve.

If children cannot understand how it feels to speak on the air, let them engage in some vigorous physical activity, and when all are panting, recite a few lines and listen to the tonal quality. Feel the words being placed on a cushion of air. Discover the feeling of

Voice Production

talking while breathing deeply; discover how the lungs feel when filled with air and how the back of the throat feels open when panting.

To avoid shallow breathing and help children gain the concept of an unexaggerated deep breath, the following exercises are useful:

1. With mouth closed, breathe in gently through the nose. Feel as if you are about to yawn or sigh. Place back of wrists on upper rib cage. Keep inhaling until you are aware of your rib cage pushing your hands outward, horizontally, away from your body. Inhale and exhale several times and feel the free movement of the rib cage.
2. Let two boys face each other with hands on shoulders. One boy exhales and then can be shoved over easily. He inhales and it is much more difficult to push him over.

    Discuss how boxers use air cushions to maintain balance. Note that they do not hold breath, but use it to maintain a cushion of air for balance. The same principles apply to the maintenance of good tonal quality.
3. a. Breathe in gently.
   b. Put one hand on diaphragm and one on rib cage. Feel diaphragm lower and rib cage spread outward and upward.
   c. This is how we "Stand tall." We stand tall in the torso section of body. We do not raise shoulders or hold awkward body positions.

Speech Difficulties

To eradicate a speech difficulty three things must take place:

1. Conductor must hear and identify cause of difficulty.
2. Choir members must hear difficulty.
3. Exercises and listening skills must be developed to eradicate difficulty.

The conductor needs to be constantly in tune with standard speech patterns so that he will not become so accustomed to the speech patterns of his class that he cannot listen to them objectively. He should endeavor to determine the cause of the difficulty and help the choir hear errors. Listening to tape recordings or hearing the teacher mimic the anomoly will help children hear themselves. Pupils may suggest ways in which the difficulty may be overcome, or the teacher may find good ideas in text books. (See listing at end of chapter.)

Some common difficulties and ways in which to correct them follow:

I. Incorrect Placement of Voice

Broad vowel placement in which all vowels seem to be produced with a wide ee sound is common with primary age children. The sound may be typified as a broadcasting voice or a playground voice. It is usually more evident in slow ponderous speech than in quick speech.

If the teacher can imitate the broad sound, pupils will begin to hear it.

Let children whistle. Repeat a spoken sentence on the whistle. Whistle again and listen to the place where the whistle sounds. Try to speak there. Children will usually say the whistle sound seems out in front and above the head.

Children must hear the difference between the two and then try to copy a narrowly vibrating vocal sound. The clear bell-tone of a true boy soprano is good to copy and listen to.

II. Audible Breath Taking

This may arise when mechanics of breathing have been unduly stressed.

Close mouth. Inhale slowly and gently to expand rib cage. Place fingers on rib cage and feel it expand slowly. Do not make any noticeable breathing sounds.

Begin several poems. Listen for audible breathing. As children learn to listen to themselves, audible breath-taking disappears.

III. Limited Range of Tone

The English language is musical and the tone ranges almost as if one were singing. Few physically normal children will be monotones in that they speak in one tone alone. Most will have a

Voice Production

few tones variation. Children with hearing loss in certain sound ranges will usually omit these ranges in speaking or singing because they cannot hear them. Children who are tone deaf will need referral to a speech clinic for specialized help.

The child with normal hearing and small range of tonal quality will profit from the following ear-training exercises:

1. Without looking at piano tell whether notes are high or low. It may take time before children actually hear high and low tones. At first they will equate concepts high and low with upper and lower sections of piano or with concepts of loud and soft. A loud high note in early ear-training will be designated low, and a soft low note, high.

   Gradually play notes closer together until children can hear differences.

   Let children sing high notes and low notes. Raise hands high on high notes and low on low notes. Stand on a chair to sing high notes. Sit on floor to sing low notes.

2. Repeat voiced and unvoiced consonants while raising hands high and low. Ask children which sound is high and which is low.

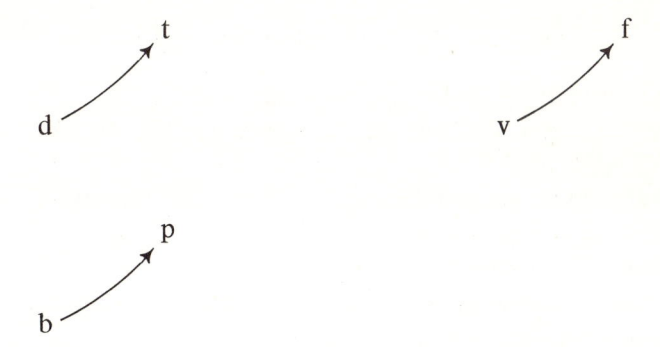

```
         t                              f
        ↗                              ↗
      d                              v

              p
             ↗
           b
```

Use repetitive spoken words to emphasize voiced and unvoiced consonants.

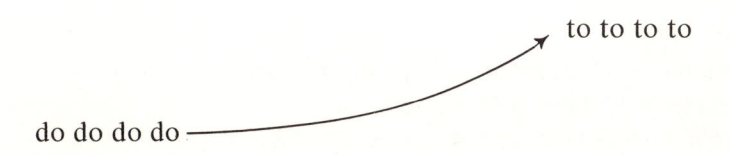

```
                              ↗ to to to to
do do do do ─────────────────
```

boy boy boy ——→ pay pay pay

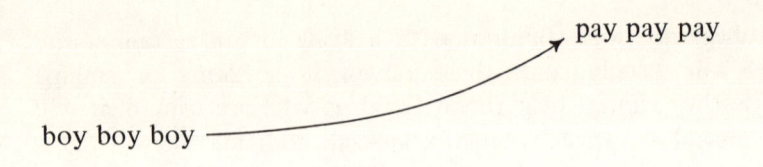

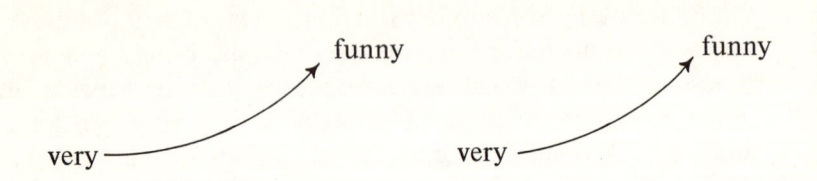

very —— ↗ funny   very —— ↗ funny

3. Listen to music and raise and lower hands as tones change pitch. Listen to speaking voices and try to do the same. Help children hear the constantly changing pitch of spoken English.
4. Recite a line of poetry. Mark high and low pitches on a copy as the child thinks he hears pitches. Try to repeat line and follow marked pitches:

Jack and Jill went up the hill OR Jack and Jill went up the hill.

5. Act out stories that contain varying voices:
   Pretend you are one of the bears in "Goldilocks and the Three Bears."
   Pretend you are the giant in "Jack and the Beanstalk."
   Pretend you are a mouse, a cow, a bird, or a cat.
   Pretend you are frightened, bold, or shy.
6. Teacher asks a question on one pitch and child answers on same or different pitch.

               My name is John.
      What is your name?   OR
               My name is John.

7. Practise singing scales to do (doh), re (rah), me (mee), fa (fah), sol (soh), la (lah), ti (tee), do (doh).
8. On a monotone count: 1,2,3. 1,2,3. 1,2,3.

Voice Production

With rising inflection count:[2]

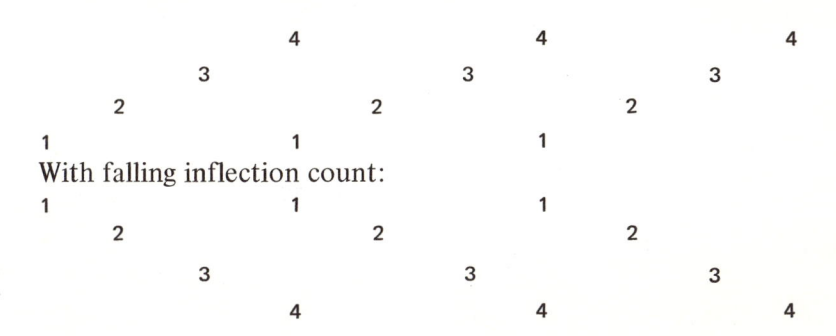

```
              4              4              4
           3              3              3
        2              2              2
     1              1              1
```

With falling inflection count:
```
     1              1              1
        2              2              2
           3              3              3
              4              4              4
```

9. Monotonous tone is often due to lack of vitality and life. Check nutritional elements in children's diets. Plenty of good vigorous physical activity outdoors in the fresh air will help pupils to have a more vital outlook and will help improve tonal qualities.

IV. Lazy Lips and Jaws

Lazy lips and jaws lead to poor articulation. Active flexible lips and jaws lead to carefully enunciated words and clearly-heard meanings. Exercises are useful to make pupils aware of active lips and to help them use lips with flexibility. However, constant development of a listening attitude by the choir is more important than exercises to develop clear articulation in normal groups of children.

Many children need to learn how to open their jaws and mouths because they speak with teeth almost closed. Play relaxing games, if possible, in front of a mirror.

1. It is bedtime. We yawn, stretch, yawn again.
2. We visit the doctor. He puts a depressor on our tongue. He says, "Open and say, Ah!"
3. Look in the mirror. Does your mouth open widely every chance it gets? Are your teeth touching all the time?

   Make a shadow on the wall of a bird with your first three fingers. Make up a conversation and see if you can open your mouth as wide as your shadow bird.

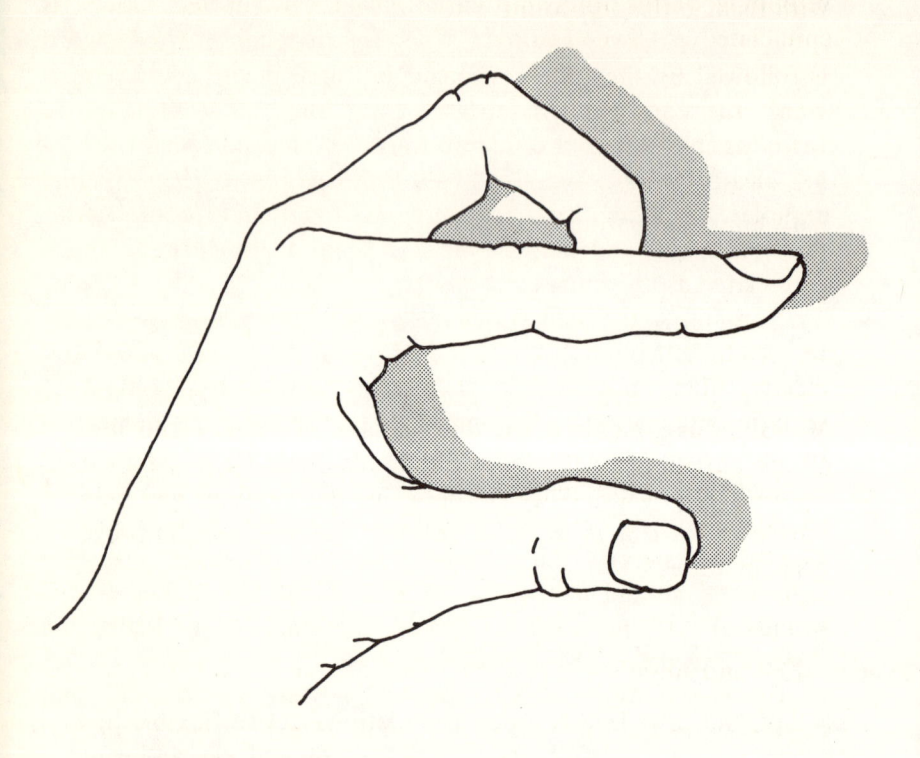

4. Gradually increase speed and open and shut mouth as quickly as possible.
5. Repeat nonsense rhymes and gradually increase speed:
   Peter Piper picked a peck of pickled peppers.
   She sells sea-shells beside the sea-shore.

V. Poorly Enunciated Words

Poor enunciation is a national habit, and through choral speaking some inroads can be made to help pupils speak more clearly. Hamlet said, "Speak the speech I pray you as I pronounce it to you trippingly on the tongue." This implies careful listening and careful enunciation.

Because words are parts of phrases and sentences and not separate sound entities in themselves, the enunciation of beginning and ending word sounds is dependent upon surrounding words. One attaches the final consonant of a word to the beginning of the following initial vowel. "Sweet and Low" is enunciated as "Sweetandlow." When the final consonat of a word is followed by the same consonant in initial position in the next word, the consonant is repeated only once. "I want to go to town" is enunciated "I wanto go to town." The consonant should be clearly enunciated so that both words together sound complete. Students tend to run words together without hearing the consonant, and neither word is heard in its entirety and is enunciated as "I wanna go to town."

Nonsense verse such as Lewis Carroll's "Jabberwocky" may be used to help pupils listen to themselves and hear each consonant clearly. Many poems lend themselves to the development of specific enunciation skills, and a file of these may be developed by the teacher. "Sweet and Low" by Alfred Lord Tennyson may be used to develop "p," "d," and "ng" enunciation skills. These sounds are often omitted in medial and ending parts of words. The "t" of "sweet," "d" of "wind," and "p" of "sleep" as ending consonants should be clearly enunciated and heard. The medial sounds of "st" in "western," "t" in "waters," "t" in "little" and "pretty" need thoughtful consideration.

Unstressed "ng" sounds should be heard in "rolling" and "dying"; and the "in" sound of "rollin' " and "dyin' " avoided.

Sweet and Low
by Alfred Tennyson[3]

Sweet and low, sweet and low,
    Wind of the western sea,
Low, low, breathe and blow,
    Wind of the western sea!
Over the rolling waters go,
Come from the dying moon, and blow,
    Blow him again to me:
While my little one, while my pretty one, sleeps.

Sleep and rest, sleep and rest,
    Father will come to thee soon:
Rest, rest, on mother's breast,
    Father will come to thee soon:
Father will come to his babe in the nest,
Silver sails all out of the west
    Under the silver moon:
Sleep, my little one, sleep, my pretty one, sleep.

Lewis Carroll "Jabberwocky," from *Through the Looking-Glass*

'Twas brillig, and the slithy toves
    Did gyre and gimble in the wabe:
All mimsy were the borogoves,
And the mome raths outgrabe.

"Beware the Jabberwock, my son!
    The jaws that bite, the claws that catch!
Beward the Jubjub bird, and shun
    The frumious Bandersnatch!"

He took his vorpal sword in hand;
    Long time the manxome foe he sought —
So rested he by the Tumtum tree,
    And stood awhile in thought.

And, as in uffish thought he stood,
    The Jabberwock, with eyes of flame,
Came whiffling through the tulgey wood,
    And burbled as it came!

One, two! One, two! And through and through
    The vorpal blade went snicker-snack!
He left it dead, and with its head
    He went galumphing back.

"And has thou slain the Jabberbock?
    Come to my arms, my beamish boy!
O frabjous day! Callooh, Callay!"
    He chortled in his joy.

'Twas brillig, and the slithy toves
    Did gyre and gimble in the wabe:
All mimsy were the borogoves,
And the mome raths outgrabe.

Reference Sources

Some reference books containing exercises, games, and ideas for the development of enunciation skills are the following:

Keppie, Elizabeth E., Conrad F. Wedberg, and Miriam Keslar. *Speech Improvement Through Choral Speaking.* Magnolia, Mass.: Expression Company, 1952.

Nemoy, Elizabeth McGinley. *Speech Correction through Story-Telling Units.* Magnolia, Mass.: Expression Company, 1954.

Scott, Louise Binder, and J.J. Thompson. *Talking Time.* St. Louis, Missouri: Webster Publishing Company, 1951.

Thomas, Charles. *Handbook of Speech Improvement.* New York: Ronald Press, 1956.

Wilcox, John C. *Voice Training for Speech and Choric Reading.* 500 Kimball Bldg., Chicago, Ill.: J.C. Wilcox, 1938.

Wood, Alice L. *Sound Games.* New York: C.P. Dutton and Company, 1948.

Footnotes

[1] Berry, Mildred Freburg, and Jon Eisenson, *Speech Disorders* (New York: Appleton-Century-Crofts, 1956), p. 297.

[2] Thurburn, Gwynneth, *Voice and Speech* (London: James Nisbet and Company, Ltd., 1939), p. 63.

[3] Tennyson, Alfred Lord, "Sweet and Low" from W.J. Rolfe, ed., *The Complete Poetical Works of Alfred Lord Tennyson* (Boston: Houghton Mifflin Company, 1898), p. 111.

[4] Carroll, Lewis, "Jabberwocky," from *Through the Looking-Glass* (London: Macmillan and Company, 1952), p. 20.

Chapter XI
THE CURTAIN RISES

Choral speaking lends itself readily to public performance. With a few extra practices, selections learned in class may be used, and unlike the singing choir, all voices may be included. Programming is flexible, and selections may be arranged in many ways. The happy team-spirit of a choral speaking choir elicits enthusiastic audience response.

Many types of programs may be used: one selection; a series joined together by narrative, music, or staging; pantomines, shadow-plays, and puppet shows with choral speaking background; or choral speaking as part of a dramatic or musical production.

Pupils should be encouraged to stand on the balls of the feet, heads high, eyes shining, faces lifted in a smile so that well-focused tone will result. Uniformity of dress aids oneness of thought. White blouses and shirts with dark skirts and trousers with perhaps ties in school colors are appropriate. Neat hairdos, even in an age of wild hairdos, are a must. Sometimes wisely-chosen costuming will enhance meanings, but costuming must not substitute for excellence of performance.

Opportunities to practise under stage conditions should be provided. Children need to become accustomed to bright lights, auditorium acoustics, and standing on risers. Constant focused attention on a director is difficult for young children to maintain over a period of time. Boys in the 9-to-12-year-old-group will tend to become dizzy if required to stand longer than three or four minutes in one position. They should be taught to flex knees and change eye focus positons. It is better to have physical movement within a program with groups moving or changing positions from time to time.

One needs to test the acoustics of any auditorium where choral speaking will take place. Many times if young children are placed on the stage proper, voices will not carry to the back of the auditorium. Risers at the front of the stage are effective and bring children into closer physical contact with the audience. Experiment with different choir placements to find best acoustics for voices. Enunciation may need to be more precise, and all selections paced slightly slower than in classroom setting.

A semi-circular arrangement is usually best with children standing and sitting on risers, chairs, cushions, or tables. If the teacher conducts from the wings of stage or from the side of the platform, various slanted arrangements are good.

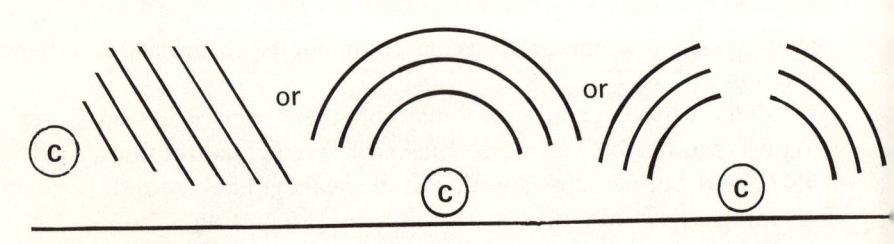

C — conductor

The voice parts may be placed physically in various ways within the choir:

I. **Standard Choral Singing Arrangement in Four Sections.**

In a choral singing choir the arrangement of the four parts is usually as follows. The placement is most acceptable in choral speaking when four differing sections are utilized.

Bass or Men's Voices	Tenor or Higher Men's Voices
Alto or Deep Women's Voices	Soprano or High Women's Voices

C

II. Three Part Arrangement

Three sections of voices may be grouped as follows:

```
H H H   M M   M L L
H H H   M M   L L L
H H M   M M   L L L
```

ⓒ

Key: H — high voices
      M — medium voices
      L — low voices
      C — conductor

III. Blended Arrangement

Two, three, four and more sections of voices may be placed alternately to produce a blending of sound. No two voice parts stand together, and students learn to blend voices with all sections as well as with their own particular section. This arrangement is effective with upper grade and experienced choirs.

```
H M H M L H M L
H L M L H M L H
L M H M L H M L
```

IV. Placement of Atypical Voices

Poor voices, monotones, stutterers, or raspy, harsh voices may be placed between good voices or in the middle of a group. Such students should be encouraged to listen to others and blend their voices with the whole tonal pattern of sound.

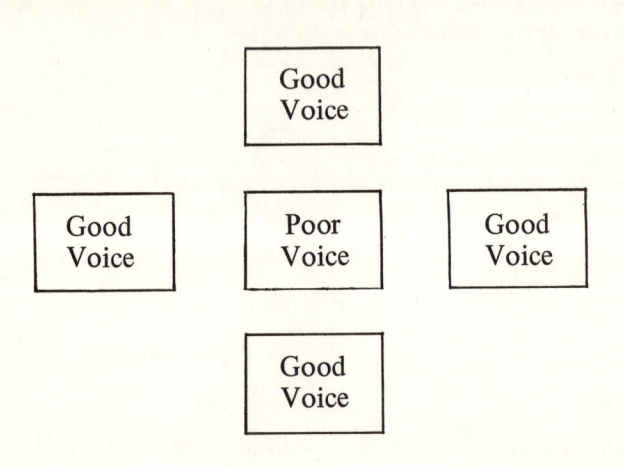

	Good Voice	
Good Voice	Poor Voice	Good Voice
	Good Voice	

V. Solo Voices

Solo voices may blend with the choir or stand apart tonally. If a blending is desired, use an X position. If the solo voice is to stand apart from the main choir, use a Y position.

```
Y O O X X O O Y
O O X X X X O O
Y O O Y Y O O Y
```

The conductor's position in a choral speaking choir should be minimized. Postion C^1 is for direct conducting and should be used with young or immature groups or with large works that need careful and constant conducting. Postion C^2 allows the audience to see choir directly and helps to enhance choir-to-audience-personal-effect. The choir should turn slightly toward conductor. Position C^3 is behind

The Curtain Rises

the curtain and is effective if choir can keep direct contact with audience while picking cues from conductor. In this position it is difficult for students to see conductor, but more control is felt than if he were not in evidence. Usually a few key students are placed where they can see conductor, and the choir follows these students. Position C^4 is in the front row of auditorium with conductor seated. This position is useful for children's groups, and it places emphasis upon children rather than upon conductor.

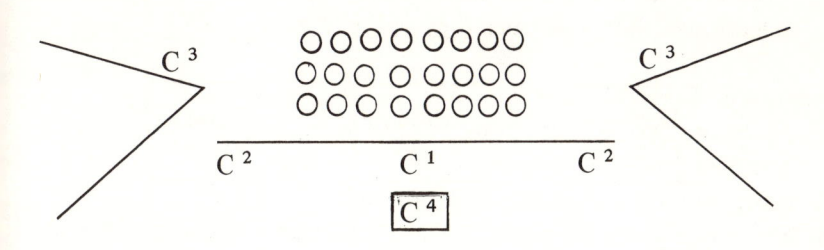

```
          C³        OOOO OOOO        C³
                    OOO O OOOO
                    OOO O OOOO
              C²         C¹         C²
                        [C⁴]
```

While preparing for public performance, help children develop their own standards of behavior and performance. These may be placed in chart form:

> We are on time.
> Our hair is combed.
> We do not chew gum.
> We do not shove.
> We keep our mouths closed in the
>   wings of the stage.
> We think about our parts.

Just before the performance:

1. Be certain everyone is ready and in right place.
2. Calm down fidgety students.
3. Keep group in an expectant attitude.

4. Practice entrance cues which they may have forgotten.
5. Talk to individuals and the group until faces reflect the mood to be conveyed: "Oh I see Andrew is looking just like Tom the Piper's Son. Are you all ready to catch that pig?"
6. If any staging has been changed since last practice, let them know differences.
7. Do not let pupils misbehave or run around.
8. If you have to wait longer than expected before a performance, tell them a story, be supplied with ideas for quiet games, or let them recite quietly their favorite choral speaking selections other than ones they will perform.

During the performance:
1. Have words of selections in front of you. You may forget even a well-learned selection!
2. Keep smiling at children. It is contagious.
3. Be positive in attitudes toward children: "How good you are!" "How well you remember!" "Isn't it fun!"
4. Keep cool, calm, and relaxed. Enjoy yourself.
5. Minimize errors. Let children know you are not upset by mistakes. When students say, "John forgot his line," reply, "Did he? I didn't notice. Didn't we tell our story well? I think the audience understood what we were saying."
6. Learn to whisper quick changes of directions to children.
7. Never let your voice be heard by the audience. The adult quality of your voice will detract from the beauty of choir's rendition.
8. Enjoy the experience! Choral speaking is fun for the teacher as well.

Chapter XII
TECHNIQUES FOR THE ADVANCED CHOIR

*Forth to high heaven let your praises ring,
But yet with caution, listen while you sing.
Let there be in you unity and peace,
Begin together and together cease.
No word or note should ever be begun
Before the former one is fitly done.
Be careful not to cut or syncopate,
Each syllable must have its proper weight,
For if you keep enunciation good
The words are rightly heard and understood.
When to the Lord you will your anthems raise
These simple maxims shall perfect your praise.
Lift up your hearts to God in love and fear,
Lift up your voices, resonant and clear,
Lift up your minds, by thinking what you say.
Not noise, but prayerful music be your way.
The cry that to the ear of God doth dart
Is cry, not of the throat, but of the heart.
            from a 14th century gradual* [1]

With advanced choirs interpretation of selections is an ever-growing creative-type of learning process. The conductor does not impose his interpretation upon the choir; instead the choir evolves patterns of interpretation that most sincerely interpret the nuances of mood and meaning inherent within selections.

The sheer artistry of the finest in choral speaking demands many skills of performers and conductors. This chapter will present some facets of interpretation that cause selections to be interpreted as works of art. The ideas should be useful to advanced conductors, skilled individual interpreters, and advanced choral groups.

The Choir

Broadening Choir's Knowledge

The conductor must do much more than present the mechanics of choral interpretation. He must develop knowledge of poetry and speech and encourage deep appreciations of written and spoken language. He should encourage true listening skills that involve all one's intellect and being so that the student becomes part of the action in the same way a baseball fan listening to a game becomes the umpire, the team, and the individual player. The baseball fan's heart beats faster, his body becomes heated, he undoes his tie, takes off his coat, swings the bat, and catches the ball. He is a true listener.

At each practice session something should be done to help pupils gain broader understandings of literature and speech. Skills may be developed in many ways:

1. Reading excerpts of selections and discussing feelings and interpretations.
2. Listening and discussing recordings of famous speeches, poetic works, and plays.
3. Listening to recordings of excellent speakers and discussing reasons for beautiful tone and meanings.
4. Recording and evaluating choir performances on tape. Which phrases have ragged endings? Where do certain voices predominate? Where are vowels lacking in lustre? Where are consonants not spoken in unison? Where is meaning distorted by poor enunciation?
5. Individual readings followed by discussions designed to help abilities of each choir member.

Role of Individual within the Choir

Discussions about the role of individual choir members should elicit some of the following guidelines.
A choir member:
1. Is individualistic, yet part of the whole.
2. Contributes ideas of interpretation.
3. Blends vocal tones with choir, but retains personal tonal colorations.

4. Enunciates carefully.
  5. Follows conductor's signals.
  6. Listens to the choir as he speaks within it.
  7. Feels the inner meaning of the selection.

Physical Attitudes

The physical attitude of a choir should reflect inner feelings. However, it is possible for choirs to feel deeply and speak meaningfully and show little physical emotion. Our modern society is one in which we learn to cover deep emotions with blank faces. Only young children will show their true feelings. Middle-grade children and teen-agers will cover feelings with a straight-faced facade and often will look glum during an exciting passage or bored while expressing a lyrical passage.

Smiling eyes and bright, interested facial expressions do not come naturally to all. Pupils may be encouraged to relate the story in their own words, or pantomine the action in order to develop freer attitudes toward interpretation. A large mirror may help pupils observe facial expressions during practice time.

Bodily movement may be used in some selections if it enhances the meaning; but if it is movement for movement's sake, or if it is distracting in any way to the listener, it should not be used.

Eye contact with an audience should be meaningful, and students should talk to the audience and look at the audience as if speaking, personally, to a friend.

The Mechanics of Interpretation

Development of Structural Awareness

The total impression of a selection for choir members and audience may be fragmentary. Wholeness, especially in long selections, must be achieved consciously.

In simple selections discussions may center about: What does the poem mean to you? What was the poet trying to say? What is the central idea of the first verse? What is the central idea of the second verse? How is the stanza related to the refrain? Does the refrain tie the stanzas together? How do the meanings of the first verse relate to those in the second?

Structural patterns of total selections help to develop the idea of wholeness. A simple structure might be shown as:

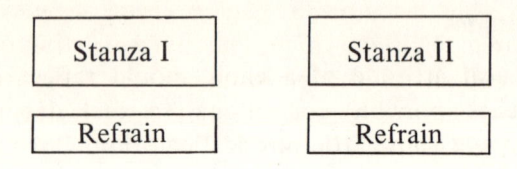

```
┌──────────┐      ┌──────────┐
│ Stanza I │      │ Stanza II│
└──────────┘      └──────────┘
┌──────────┐      ┌──────────┐
│ Refrain  │      │ Refrain  │
└──────────┘      └──────────┘
```

Involved structures may be sketched, and thought images of each section discussed:

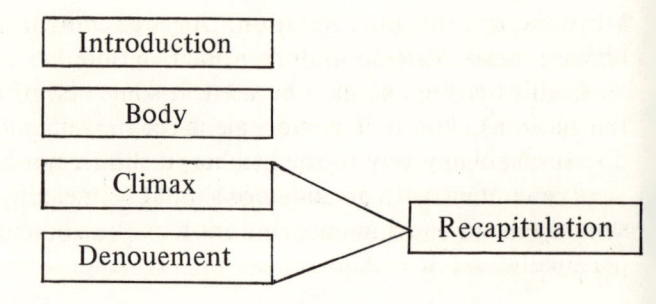

```
┌──────────────────┐
│   Introduction   │
└──────────────────┘
┌──────────────────┐
│       Body       │
└──────────────────┘
┌──────────────────┐
│      Climax      │──┐
└──────────────────┘  │    ┌──────────────────┐
┌──────────────────┐  ├───▶│  Recapitulation  │
│    Denouement    │──┘    └──────────────────┘
└──────────────────┘
```

The meaning will be clear to listeners if all choir members have a progressing mental picture of each section as it is repeated. To help develop a progressing mental picture, children may draw pictures of each section, write the story in their own words, and interpret sections with pantomine or physical movement of various types. Older students may mentally imagine pictures for each section in their minds only. To cause the selection to move forward as a whole, climaxes may be marked in the score so that the thought and tone surge from one climax point to another.

Technique for the Advanced Choir

The Relationship of Meter and Meaning

In both poetry and music the interpreter must find the correct balance between meter and meaning. In a musical selection performed by a young child who has had an overdose of metrical counting, a metronomic type of music with heavy emphasis upon the "one" beat is the usual result. Each measure of music resounds with ONE-two-three, ONE-two-three. The rhythmic structure becomes the be-all and end-all of the performance. In a metronomic-type of interpretation there is almost complete loss of the total picture or meaning of the selection.

The true musician will hear the rhythm of 1-2-3 in a different setting. He may hear a pattern of 1-2-3-4-5-6-7-8-9-10-11-12 and then another pattern of 1 - 2 - 3 - 4 - 5 - 6 followed by 1-2-3-4-5-6-7-8-9-10-11-12-13-14-15. Both novice and musician will be reading the same 1-2-3 time signature, but the musician will hear rhythm as one part of the whole, whereas the novice will be so busy counting the trees, he will never discover that the trees make up a beautiful forest.

Similar principles apply to the interpretation of poetry. The novice tends to rely upon the beat or number of feet in the line instead of seeing meter in relation to the total picture of a beautiful forest in which one finds trees numbered 1-2-3.

In the following stanza the metrical interpretation is noted in I and the artistic interpretation in II. The artist would see the rhythmic understructure as an aid to meaning, as part of the whole, as large waves of rhythm, rather than narrowly-measured entities.

from "Indian Children" by Annette Wynne

I. Metrical Interpretation

    ONE /   / two / three   / four
1. Where we walk to school each day

    ONE /   / two / three / four
2. Indian children used to play

    ONE /   / two /three/ four
3. All about our native land

    ONE /   / two   /three / four
4. Where the shops and houses stand.

II. Meter and Meaning Balanced

    1 /   2 /   3 /   4 /
1. Where we walk to school each day
    5 /   6 /   7 /   8 /
2. Indian children used to play
    9 / 10 /   11 / 12 /
3. All about our native land
   13 /   14 /   15 /   16 /
4. Where the shops and houses stand.

Notice the sweep of interpretation II. The meaning is in a phrase of 16 beats. This could be divided into two phrases of eight and eight according to individual preference. However, the interpreter does not lose the four-foot line, but subordinates this to the larger meaning of the selection. Creative interpretation gives meaning the most important role and interprets rhythm and meter in relationship to meaning.

Run-on-Lines

There are two approaches to run-on lines, free and metrical. If a free approach is desired, run-on-lines may read as prose with no noticeable break between lines: "Sing a song of Scissor men Sitting in the sun."[3] If a metrical approach is desired, the regular rhythmical beat of line must be followed:

>Sing a song of Scissor men
>Sitting in the sun.

Structural Patterns

The most-used structural patterns in choral speaking are unison, solo with refrain, two-part work such as dialogue or antiphonal response, line-a-child or sequential, part speaking and part speaking with group responses. The two most difficult structures are unison and line-a-child. Line-a-child is difficult for young children because they must come in exactly on time. Children should know the complete poem before parts are assigned, and then they will read their own line as if it were part of the whole poem, rather than a separate entity. Many children should be given the opportunity to recite, and a line should not be assigned permanently to one child.

Technique for the Advanced Choir

Mature choirs and older students will enjoy practising line-a-child poems in which they begin to speak a moment before the end of the preceding line. The "toppling effect" of one line overlapping another produces marvelous climax points, as line upon line builds to the point of highest meaning. The exact pacing for a toppling effect is dependent upon the type of selection as well as upon the creativity and interpretational mood of the participants.

Unison speaking is dependent upon many voices blending as one. To do this well, each person must be able to hear his own voice and the voices of those near him blending into a common oneness of tone. It is unlikely that young or immature choirs can achieve beauty of expression in long unison-type selections.

The biggest problem in unison work is heavy, labored speech and monotonous tone caused by many inexperienced voices lumbering through words with little emphasis upon meaning or tonal coloration. Some of the following ideas are useful during unison practice sessions:

1. Conduct in long, sweeping phrases.
2. Speak softly, lightly, and quickly.
3. Break the selection into parts and utilize line-a-child or antiphonal structures.
4. Discuss meaning and tone coloration.
5. Divide class into groups to work out group ideas of expression and nuance.
6. Ask individuals to repeat selections in their own way, using their own special tone colorations.
7. If selection becomes too heavy and labored, do not practise it for a while. Intersperse unison selections with other types of structure.
8. Sing a light quick song before practising, or do some vigorous physical exercises.
9. Practise listening to each other and following conductor's movements exactly until unity of articulation and syllabification is achieved.
10. Practise beginnings and endings until all voices are together and the work is clean-cut and precise.
11. Accurate memorization of words and technical detail is necessary for precision.

Tonal Qualities

Musical Ideas

Ideas from music may be incorporated into choral speaking:
1. Selections may be thought of as in a major or minor key.
2. The harmonic structuring of voices may be utilized for tonal effects:
    (a) Heavy voices combined with light voices.
    (b) Blends of alto, soprano, tenor, or bass in groups or individually may be used.
    (c) One voice type may be used against a background of opposite voice types.
3. The choir may be encouraged to listen to itself as an orchestra with the high, light voices representing the woodwinds and violins, and the deep voices as double basses, drums, and brasses. High, light voices are good for questioning passages, and low deep voices lend themselves to big sounds or sounds in a minor key.
4. Stretti of voices is useful at climax points.
5. Variations of fugue form may be used at beginning and ending of selections:
    (a) Beginning: VOICE IV _____

                              VOICE III _____

                    VOICE II _____

         VOICE I _____

    (b) Ending:
         <u>all voices</u>

         _____

         _____

         _____

Begin a selection softly and build each line, little by little, to a loud finale, or begin strongly and gradually die away to a whisper. Try blending various parts into trios, duos, and quartets utilizing fugue form.
6. Counterpoint ideas:
   (a) One voice speaks while another voice or voices at another pitch repeat phrases or nonsense syllables.
   (b) Two voices or two groups of voices with distinctive tonal colorings may repeat the same words.
   (c) A group of voices speaks in a monotone with regularly inflected voices as solo, group, or complete choir superimposed upon it.
   (d) Choirs should be able to speak in legato manner as well as staccato. Practice exercises with nonsense rhymes are good.

Ways of Developing Varying Tone

There is a dichotomy in the tonal quality of choral speaking. All voices must have common interpretational patterns of rhythm, mood, inflection, and enunciation; but voices must not imitate. Each voice should be part of the whole, but with individual variations. Each group will have a group pitch, but each voice in the group will rise and fall individually around the group pitch. If pupils imitate one another in tonal quality, the beauty of varied pitches around a central group pitch is lost and the result is an "elocution-type" sound. Individuality within the framework of unity is the goal.

Pupils should be encouraged to:

1. Listen to their own voice within the framework of the whole choir.
2. Realize the value of individual interpretation and tonal coloring to the whole.
3. Listen to the striated sound produced by the dichotomy of individual and group patterns. Voices 1, 2, and 3 are all soprano voices with similar inflectional and tonal colorations. The blending of these produces an over-all average effect. On this average perhaps no single voice will fall, but all will cluster around it.

3 soprano voices

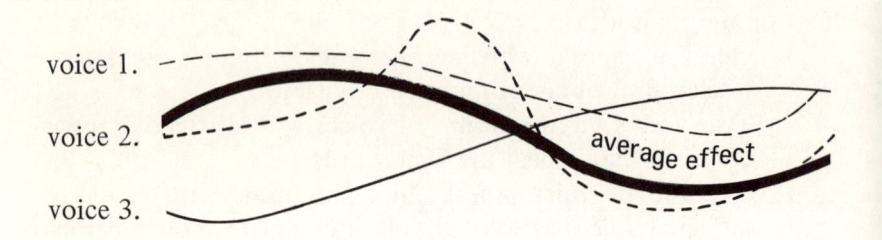

voice 1.
voice 2.
voice 3.

average effect

4. Understand that in singing all voices are on the same note at a given instant, but in choral speaking all voices are within range of the same tone. It is this range, even within similar parts, that causes rich, spoken group tone colorations.
5. Inflectional patterns must arise from the voices within the choir and should not be artificially imposed.

Footnotes

[1] Lyon, James, *Notes on Choral Speaking* (Toronto: Clarke, Irwin and Company, Ltd., 1941), p. 33.

[2] Noyes, Alfred, "A Song of Sherwood," *Collected Poems* (Philadelphia, Penn.: J.B. Lippincott Company, 1941), p. 10.

[3] Nightingale, Madeline, "The Scissor-Man," from *Nursery Lays for Nursery Days* (London: Oxford Press: Basil Blackwell and Mott, Ltd., 1940), p. 42.

[4] Noyes, *op. cit.*, p. 25.

BIBLIOGRAPHY

Abney, Louise. *Choral Speaking Arrangements for the Upper Grades.* Magnolia, Mass.: Expression Co., 1952.

Anderson, Paul S. *Language Skills in Elementary Education.* New York: The Macmillan Co., 1964.

Arbuthnot, May Hill. *The Arbuthnot Anthology of Children's Literature.* Chicago: Scott, Foresman and Co., 1961.

Arnstein, Flora J. *Poetry in the Elementary Education.* New York: Appleton-Century-Crofts, 1962.

Bender, James F., and Victor M. Kleinfeld. *Principles and Practices of Speech Correction.* New York: Pitman Publishing Corp., 1938.

Berry, Mildred Freburg, and Jon Eisenson. *Speech Disorders.* New York: Appleton-Century-Crofts, Inc., 1956.

Brown, Helen A., and Harry J. Heltman. *Teaching Guidebook for Use with Read Together Poems.* Elmsford, New York: Row Peterson and Company, 1961.

Cunningham, Cornelius Carman. *Making Words Come Alive.* Dubuque, Iowa: Wm. C. Brown Co., 1951.

De Banke, Cecile. *The Art of Choral Speaking.* Boston: Baker's Plays, 1937.

De Witt, Marguerite E. *Practical Methods in Choral Speaking.* Boston: Expression Co., 1936.

Dolman, John. *The Art of Reading Aloud.* New York: Harper and Row, 1956.

Enfield, Gertrude. *Verse Choir Values and Techniques.* Boston: Expression Co., 1937.

Finn, William Joseph. *The Art of the Choral Conductor.* Boston: C. C. Birchard and Co., 1939.

Grauman, Helen G. *Music in my Bible.* Mountain View, Calif.: Pacific Press Publishing Assoc., 1956.

Gullan, Marjorie. *Choral Speaking.* London: Methuen and Co., Ltd., 1936.

Gullan, Marjorie. *The Speech Choir.* New York: Harper and Brothers, 1937.

Hamm, Agnes Curren. *Choral Speaking Techniques.* Milwaukee, Wisconsin: The Tower Press, 1951.

Harvel, Dorothy, and May Williams Ward. *An Approach to Social Studies through Choral Speaking.* Boston: Expression Company Publishers, 1945.

Hemphill, Edith Irene. *Choral Speaking and Speech Improvement.* Darien, Conn.: Educational Publishing Corp., 1945.

Henneke, Ben Graf. *Reading Aloud Effectively.* New York: Rinehart and Co., 1956.

Hicks, Helen Gertrude. *The Reading Chorus.* New York: Noble and Noble Publishers, Inc., 1939.

Jones, Archie Neff. *Techniques in Choral Conducting.* Cooper Square, New York: Carl Fischer, Inc., 1948.

Keppie, Elizabeth, Evangeline. *The Teaching of Choric Speech.* Boston: Expression Co., 1932.

_____. *Speech Improvement through Choral Speaking* (for Primary Grades). Boston: Expression Co., 1932.

Bibliography

_____, and Conrad F. Wedberg, and Miriam Kessler. *Speech Improvement through Choral Speaking.* Magnolia, Mass.: Expression Co., 1952.

Library of Congress, Music Department, recordings of poets.

Lyon, James. *Notes on Choral Speaking.* Toronto: Clarke Irwin and Co., Ltd., 1941.

Mitchell, Lucy Sprague. *Another Here and Now.* New York: E. P. Dutton and Co., Inc., 1937.

Nemoy, Muriel B. *Speech Correction through Story-Telling Units.* Magnolia, Mass.: Expression Co., 1954.

Newton, Muriel B. *The Unit Plan for Choral Reading.* Boston: Expression Co., 1938.

Rasmussen, Carrie. *Choral Speaking for Speech Improvement.* Magnolia, Mass.: Expression Co., 1953.

Rehner, Herbert Adrian. *The Dramatic Use of Oral Interpretation and Choral Speaking.* New York: Bruce-Howard Publishing House, 1951.

Scherchen, Herman. *Handbook of Conducting.* London: Oxford University Press, 1951.

Scholes, Percy A. *The Oxford Companion to Music.* New York: Oxford University Press, 1950.

Scott, Louise Binder, and J. J. Thompson. *Talking Time.* St. Louis, Missouri: Webster Publishing Co., 1955.

Smith, Joseph Fielding, and James R. Linn. *Skill in Reading Aloud.* New York: Harper and Row, 1960.

Swann, Mona. *An Approach to Choral Speech.* London: Macmillan Co., 1949.

Thurburn, Gwynneth, Loviday. *Voice and Speech.* London: James Nisbet and Co., Ltd., 1939.

Tippett, James S. *A World to Know.* New York: Harper & Row, 1961.

Walsh, Gertrude. *Sing Your Way to Better Speech.* New York: E. P. Dutton and Co., Inc., 1955.

Wilcox, John C. *Voice Training for Speech and Choric Reading.* 500 Kimball Bldg., Chicago: J. C. Wilcox, 1938.